"Ten months after Ronald Reagan's landslide re-election victory in 1984, David Stockman finally resigned as the president's budget director to write his own book. His memoir, THE TRIUMPH OF POLITICS, *concentrated on the same pivotal events which I originally described in* THE EDUCATION OF DAVID STOCKMAN AND OTHER AMERICANS, *and confirmed my own sense of the chaos and fateful error. . . . Despite the controversy, I always envisioned it as a dispassionate narrative of how politics and policy-making always interact in government, a case study of how Washington really works."*—William Greider

"The article that created the furor around Stockman. . . . In addition, Greider writes of the repercussions of the interview and delivers a thoughtfully streetwise essay on the problems of supply-side economics and the effects of the political process on the American economic system."

—*Chicago Tribune*

"There is no better journalist in America than William Greider. His portrait of the eternal clash between the dream and the power in politics . . . will endure to instruct future generations in the Byzantine difficulties of government." —Russell Baker

"THE ESSENTIAL BOOK ON WASHINGTON TODAY." —Anthony Lewis, *The New York Times*

WILLIAM GREIDER worked at the *Washington Post* for fourteen years. In 1980 Greider began the nine months of periodic conversations with David Stockman that culminated in the famous *Atlantic* article. He is currently national news editor of *Rolling Stone*.

THE
EDUCATION OF
David Stockman
AND
Other Americans

William Greider

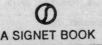

A SIGNET BOOK

NEW AMERICAN LIBRARY

A portion of this book first appeared in *The Atlantic*.

For my mother and father

Contents

Preface to
the Revised Edition

Ten months after Ronald Reagan's landslide reelection victory in 1984, David Stockman finally resigned as the President's budget director to write his own book. His memoir, *The Triumph of Politics*, concentrated on the same pivotal events of 1981, which I had originally described in *The Education of David Stockman and Other Americans*, and confirmed my own sense of the chaos and fateful error.

The triumphant reelection of Ronald Reagan in 1984 would seem to contradict my narrative of political failure (and Stockman's gloomy account of "fiscal disaster"). Most Americans probably believe that the President's promises were fulfilled, albeit belatedly and after a long, severe recession. The enormous federal deficits continue, but nothing disastrous seems to have resulted. The wiser leaders in Congress know better, which is why they keep struggling to correct the disorder that was created back in 1981.

In a sense, Americans have already suffered for the Reagan deficits, and the painful consequences have been unevenly distributed. The fiscal imbalance, combined with a restrained monetary policy, produced an uneven economic recovery undermined by historically unprecedented interest rates and dependence on foreign lenders to absorb the burgeoning government debt. The result was below-average growth in the national output and personal incomes, the persistence of high unemployment, devastation for export industries, rising debt burdens for business and consumers, and continuing waves of bankruptcy even though the economy is supposedly healthy. This damage was less dramatic and visible than the financial crisis that Stockman and others predicted, but the costs are real for millions of American workers and enterprises. As long as huge deficits continue, the threat of worse consequences continues too.

I have added only minor revisions and updating for this edition because, five years later, it is even more obvious that the political events I described in 1981 formed a crucial watershed. The original illusions and deceptions of the "Reagan Revolution" produced the disorder that will preoccupy the federal government throughout the 1980s. Governing by illusion may succeed in pushing basic problems off into the future, but it does not make them disappear.

Despite the partisan controversy that originally surrounded my story of David Stockman, I always envisioned it as a dispassionate narrative of how politics and policymaking always interact in government, a case study of how Washington really works. It pleases me that in scores of colleges and universities around the country professors of political science, public administration, and economics are assigning the text for that purpose, as a story that teaches. The original lessons still seem to apply.

—William Greider
March 1986

Publisher's Note

By the autumn of 1981, barely nine months into his presidency, Ronald Reagan was already entrapped by messy realities. His visionary notions of laissez-faire conservatism were tattered by compromise and his inflated campaign promises were already in collision with contradictory developments. Instead of the new era of prosperity which Reagan had promised, the national economy was in recession again, a long and painful one which would push unemployment to its highest level since the early 1940s. Instead of a balanced budget, Reagan's novel three-year tax-cut had created a future of horrendous federal deficits. These contradictions were becoming clear to the governing elite of policymakers and politicians in Washington, if not to the general public, when a bizarre thing happened, a random event that crystallized their doubts and broadcast their private fears to the entire nation.

Out of nowhere, it seemed, David A. Stockman, the young and skillful Director of Management and Budget in the Reagan Cabinet, was in the newspaper headlines and on the television news—revealing his own doubts about the Reagan program and his fears of failure. Ronald Reagan's economic recovery program—of which Stockman was a principal architect—wasn't working, he conceded. Stockman had become known to the public as the zealous point man for Reagan's fiscal revolution; now he was making the most astonishing confessions. The celebrated budget reductions, enacted by Congress only a few months before, were illusory and inadequate, Stockman said. The doctrine of "supply-side" economics, which the President had embraced as justification for his across-the-board tax reductions, was naïvely optimistic, he complained. Besides, the supply-side theory merely disguised the old Republican doctrine of "trickle down" economics—helping the rich instead of the poor. The Reagan defense budget, which would more than double, and would consume $1.6 trillion in the next five years, was bloated with waste, the budget director allowed. The new legislation which reduced federal taxes for business corporations represented out-of-control greed and special-interest favors. Finally, Stockman admitted with shocking candor that even he, the bright young technocrat of the federal budget, did not fully grasp all the budget numbers. They were out of control, he said, and the prospect for fiscal control was not especially bright.

The startling revelations created a storm of controversy, first in Washington, then across the nation, as people absorbed the news accounts and listened to the political reactions. Some members of Congress, including some of Stockman's Republican allies, demanded his resignation. Some Democrats insisted that they could never again believe any budget numbers Stockman told them. Editorial cartoonists mocked him. The nimble young tactician who had dazzled the public with his quick mind was now transformed to fool or knave. Stockman offered his resignation, but the President declined it.

More important to the Reagan Administration, Stockman's candid talk laid bare the inner flaws in the President's budget and tax program. It exposed the ongoing private debate among the President's own advisers and defined in brutal terms the genuine problems which Congress and the President would have to confront in the years ahead. The program wasn't working, a realization which had been perceived only dimly until Stockman spoke. His truth-telling, in short, permanently altered the way in which everyone, from rival political leaders to ordinary citizens, would look at Ronald Reagan and his administration, a turning point in his presidency.

Yet most Americans, it is safe to say, never actually read what Stockman was telling them. They depended upon truncated news accounts and short-handed quotations derived from a lengthy article in the *Atlantic* magazine, entitled. "The Education of David Stockman," by William Greider. The author was an editor at the *Washington Post* who conducted many months of private interviews with the budget director in order to produce a comprehensive account of how the Reagan Administration's economic policies developed in the opening year of his presidency. "The Education of David Stockman" is a narrative of political action, with overtones of tragedy, as the idealistic young conservative reformer discovers the complexities of the political system and watches as his moral principles are undermined by the necessities of compromise. At a major turning point of history, it conveys the operational truth about how government and politics function in Washington.

Other Americans, particularly students of government, will learn from his experience too. The account of Stockman's education in office is published here as the core material for a casebook on the realities of the modern presidency. As the author explores the deeper messages contained in the full narrative, it should become clear that the Reagan Administration's lapses and misjudgments were not at all unique. The flaws revealed by Stockman and his colleagues merely magnify flaws which are inherent in the way modern Presidents and contemporary Washington look upon their own ability to govern. Until these messages are absorbed, both by the governors and the governed, politicians who become Presidents are likely to reenact similar dramas, well after Reagan and Stockman are gone from power.

The author's essay, likewise, explores fundamental weaknesses in the way the press approaches the action of government in Washington, weaknesses which help explain why newspaper readers were so shocked by Stockman's comments. The daily news coverage travels over surfaces of words and events, but it rarely reaches deeper to the underlying reality of how things actually happen. Its own conventions and reflexes, in large measure, prevent the news media from doing more. Until this changes too, citizens will continue to be confused by the daily slices of news from Washington. Periodically, they will continue to be shocked by occasional comprehensive revelations of what's really happening, deeper accounts which explain the events they thought they understood.

Finally, this examination offers several modestly encouraging insights for ordinary citizens, at least for those who still believe in the potential of our democracy. Until citizens get a clear fix on the messy realities of their government, they are vulnerable to the same illusions which regularly mislead Presidents. On the other hand, if the public begins to comprehend the frailties of Washington experts and the accidental context in which all government policy is made, this knowledge might be empowering, encouraging citizens to take popular action and compete for power with those who have it. David Stockman's education, in short, ought to educate other Americans, too.

Introduction

As the author of that notorious article on David Stockman, I confess that I was educated, too, by the experience. I assumed that Stockman's candor would provoke political controversy, enraging his political opponents and embarrassing the Reagan Administration, but I was not prepared for the full tempest which followed. I learned, first of all, what every experienced politician already knows: the whirling eye of the news media is an uncontrollable organism which creates its own eccentric versions of what happens. After many years as a reporter, asking and demanding that other people explain themselves, I found myself suddenly on the receiving end and I felt a bit queasy (public officials might say this would be good medicine for every reporter to take). Many of the inquiring reporters were in too much of a hurry to read the article themselves so they wanted me to summarize it for them over the telephone (I winced at the memory of having done the same myself on occasion). All of them asked the same questions, not about the content, but about the personalities involved. Why did Stockman do it? Why did he tell you all those things? Some of them asked: why did *you* do it? How could you save all those sensational nuggets for so many months and not print them in the daily newspaper? I would try to explain the "ground rules" under which the interviews had taken place and the context of Stockman's agreement. But it soon became clear to me, as every politician must already understand, that complicated explanations do not hold up well if the inquiring reporter is seeking something brief and pithy. It *was* an education.

Even more painful were the news accounts in the press and on television describing the article's contents. I watched—with what can only be called wry innocence—as the daily news reports made their brutal summaries of what I had written. A long and complex narrative, constructed to preserve subtlety and ambiguity, was swiftly rendered into tart little capsules, the choicest nuggets of "news" which might provoke and embarrass. I could hardly quarrel with the accuracy of the technique (having practiced it myself for many years), but it disappointed me. I had expected, after the original flurry of reaction and controversy, that some attention might be given to the deeper questions raised by Stockman's account of governing. A practicing politician would say that I was remarkably naïve.

Thus I was confronted with a brief personal glimpse of the qualities in the news media that trouble its more thoughtful critics—the relentless factuality, the haste, the transient attention that obscures meaning even as the media deliver the daily blizzard of startling information. In time, as I pondered the reactions, I came to realize that perhaps this episode revealed something deeper about the press, a contradiction in its own reflexes and behavior that helps to explain why the news from Washington seems so confusing and, indeed, uncommunicative to many Americans. As a participant, I was right in the middle of that contradiction (or on both sides of it) and perhaps this allows me to see and describe the weakness more clearly. It has to do with the operating conventions that press and public officials have accepted among themselves, each for their own ends, and how those conventions serve only a very limited market—the elite audience of government insiders—while obscuring things for the larger audience of ordinary citizens. There are self-imposed barriers built into the daily news that diminish the quality of reality that is conveyed. The Stockman narrative leaped over those fences and inadvertently revealed the inadequacies of what gets told on a daily basis.

In the original storm of controversy, David Stockman had lunch with the President; he apologized for his indiscretions and offered his resignation. The President kept him on, however, and Stockman served as budget director until August 1985, struggling unsuccessfully for four years to undo the damage done in 1981. His trip to the Oval Office, Stockman said, was "more in the nature of a visit to the woodshed after supper." (My own visit to the "woodshed" was less dramatic; it took the form of a general chorus from the news media that I had betrayed the sacred principles of news—*Editor Scoops Own Paper*, as one headline put it.)

The news eventually turned to other matters without noting the irony that the new public issues before Washington were the same ones that Stockman had identified in the interviews: the budget crisis created by the legislation Congress had just enacted.

In his appearance before the White House press, Stockman provided a mild and generous account of what had happened in our arrangement. ". . . I think there's been some misunderstanding. Bill Greider is an old friend of mine and has been a long-time intellectual adversary. We have—what has occurred here is simply an honest but rather large misunderstanding as to the terms of the relationship we had. I understood it to be off-the-record. He understood it to be off-the-record for uses in the newspaper over the period in which our conversations occurred. It's a misunderstanding, but it is not an act of bad faith on his side nor on mine. Sometimes large misunderstandings occur in life with very unfortunate and tragic effects. And I think this is one of them.''

I appreciated his generosity but I did not think there was a misunderstanding. Neither, it seems fair to note, did many of those familiar with the ways of Washington. Experienced politicians and reporters found it implausible that a ranking public official would participate in so many lengthy tape-recorded interviews (eighteen in all) and afterward pose for photographs, and yet continue to believe that he would not be quoted by name. In any case, Stockman's flattering references to me—an ''old friend'' and ''long-time intellectual adversary''—stimulated some exotic theorizing about his psychological motivations. Stockman, it was suggested in an article by one curb-stone analyst, was perhaps enthralled by the relationship, using the sympathetic presence of an older journalist as a confessional, a place to speak forbidden truths and seek personal expiation for the sins of Reagonomics. Or was he trying to rewrite history in advance? Others saw it in slightly more lofty terms: here were two serious students of government, drawn together by mutual respect and a zest for intellectual combat, holding their own private series of earnest seminars on the fate of the federal government. I rather liked that last explanation; it made us sound so noble. My wife, who has never met David Stockman but understands me well enough, brought me back to earth. ''Come on,'' she says. ''It was two naughty little boys breaking the rules to see if they could get away with it.''

She was right, of course, about the psychology. Both Stockman and I, operating from our different roles, had done the unexpected and effectively ignored the prevailing, unwritten conventions which govern the behavior of both press and politicians in Washington. This was offensive, in different ways, to both fraternities, though Stockman endured considerably more criticism than I did. Together, we violated the standard operating context in which public officials communicate through the press. By talking honestly, Stockman contradicted the rhetorical claims and slogans which his own colleagues were offering for their program. By recounting Stockman's genuine thoughts in a comprehensive manner, I was effectively refuting the simple and shallow version of reality that the news created in its daily slices.

To understand this, however, one has to appreciate that neither of us entered into our unique arrangement with the expressed intention of changing the "rules" or even offending them. I emphasize this homely point: at the outset, Stockman and I were participating in a fairly routine transaction of Washington, a form of submerged communication which takes place with utter regularity between selected members of the press and the highest officials of government. Our mutual motivation, despite our different interests, was crassly self-serving. It did not need to be spelled out between us. I would use him and he would use me. The fancy name for this is symbiosis, which perhaps gives it more dignity than it deserves, but symbiosis is an elementary mode of operation in the ecology of Washington affairs. Whether it exists between politicians and reporters, lobbyists and congressmen, bureaucrats and private interest groups, the functional politics of the city involves complicated webs of such informal relationships, transactions for sharing access and information which go largely unobserved.

In the fall of 1980, after Ronald Reagan's dramatic election victory, when it became clear to me that Reagan would launch a powerful offensive against the status quo and that Stockman was his likely choice for the pivotal role of budget director, I suggested to Stockman that we begin meeting regularly to discuss "off the record" the flow of events in which he would be a leading participant. I appealed to his sense of history. I invoked our mutual interest in the largest questions of the modern welfare state and the conservative reform movement of which he was a leading voice. I promised that he would not be quoted in the daily newspaper; the material would be saved for comprehensive treatment at a later time when we both agreed it was appropriate. My obligation would be to produce a full and serious account of Stockman's narrative, an honest piece that would respect the complexity of the subject (an obligation I believe I kept).

Stockman accepted and we began our periodic conversations, usually every other week, over nine months. I would call his office on Friday afternoon and ask if I was on the schedule. We had an early breakfast at the Hay-Adams Hotel across Lafayette Park from the White House. In time, when the waiters saw me enter with my tape recorder, they would turn down the Musak so the background music would not intrude on my recordings of our conversations. Stockman and I were "old friends" only in the limited social usage of Washington, where anyone who has met someone twice at dinner parties is apt to call him an "old friend." We did not socialize together or play tennis on Saturday mornings, but we had known each other for several years. As a reporter, I first sought him out when he was a bright young congressman from Michigan. I had been attracted by his brilliant critiques of moderate liberalism, published in the *Public Interest* and elsewhere. Later, as an editor, I commissioned several provocative articles by him for the *Washington Post*'s Sunday edition. Stockman understood that I agreed with some essential elements of his political analysis, particularly on the incoherence and corrupting reflexes of interest-group liberalism; he also knew well enough, from my own articles and questions, that I was skeptical of the laissez-faire conservatism which he espoused, unpersuaded that it was the future.

This spirit of amiable disagreement informed our conversations, but the talk was hardly like an academic seminar. I asked questions and he answered them, a reporter interviewing a government official. What happened last week? What is going to happen next week? As the political events of 1981 grew more complicated and diffuse, we had less and less time for philosophical asides. The congressional budget process is a fiendishly difficult story in any season and interviewing David Stockman on fiscal policy at season and interviewing David Stockman on fiscal policy at 7:30 A.M. is a daunting experience. The conservative columnist George Will, who also breakfasted with the budget director, described the feeling: "When I said something dumb about the decline of productivity, he rolled his eyes heavenward and indicated that productivity is a complex subject that I should leave to the adults. He says such things agreeably, like a Gatling gun that has studied with Dale Carnegie."

This arrangement, of course, gave me several critical advantages which are not usually available to working reporters in search of daily news. I did not have to rush into print with what Stockman told me. I could wait to see whether events confirmed or refuted his opinions. I could examine the continuity of his narrative at leisure, reminding him in July of what he had predicted in February. The political calculations made in the spring were not past, splintered events that occurred and disappeared; the mistakes made in April flowed naturally into the gloom felt in September. At the outset, naturally, neither of us could have predicted the paradox which the finished writing would describe: a season of stunning legislative victories by the President which trapped him in an awesome fiscal crisis.

Actually, neither of us was really thinking about the form the writing would take. I had established a valuable peephole on the inner policy debates of the new administration. And the young budget director had established a valuable connection with an important newspaper. I would get a jump on the unfolding strategies and decisions. He would be able to prod and influence the focus of our coverage, to communicate his views and positions under the cover of our "off the record" arrangement, to make known harsh assessments that a public official would not dare to voice in the more formal settings of a press conference, speech, or "on the record" interview. Neither of us ever discussed this aspect of our communication directly. But, after the first few sessions, it was established as the implicit, sometimes even dominant business at the breakfast table. He was using me and I was using him. I did say that it was crass.

Outsiders will ask: if these talks were truly "off the record," how could the contents be useful to the *Washington Post?* Under the informal rules that the Washington press obeys, "off the record" means, first, that the public official cannot be quoted either directly or indirectly on what he has said. The information may not be used; it cannot even be attributed anonymously to an unnamed "administration official." The "off the record" interview is still valuable to a reporter, however, partly because it usually provides an unvarnished and relaxed glimpse of what a public official really thinks. The Secretary of State may be optimistic in his public declarations, but privately he is gloomy. In official utterances, the White House spokesman may deny a problem which the ubiquitous "senior officials" are privately acknowledging. The "off the record" conversations provide guidance, context, and, sometimes, the truth about matters.

But a skillful reporter can also get much of the information into the newspaper or broadcast. First, the reporter can seek out the same information elsewhere; if the substance is confirmed independently from other sources, then the reporter is free to write it, without violating the ethical strictures of "off the record." Sources understand this as well as reporters do; government officials who genuinely wish to keep a secret will begin by not discussing it with any reporters, regardless of the ground rules. Second, the skillful reporter will negotiate with his or her "off the record" source. If the interviewer hears something compelling and newsworthy, he may ask the source if that particular information can be put "on background." Under the Washington rules, "on background" means that the information can be used if attributed to an unnamed source vaguely identified as authoritative. Thus are born the "senior White House official," "the State Department adviser," and the "key congressional aide." Sometimes, an especially sensitive source will haggle over the precise anonymous attribution which is to be given to his remarks, worried that discerning readers, other members of the governing elite, will be able to puzzle out his true identity. Thus, an aide to the President may insist that he be labeled "an administration official" but not "a senior White House aide." On other occasions, a source will reflect on what he has said "off the record" and agree that his remarks can be re-classified as "on the record," directly attributed by name.

Almost from the start, Stockman and I bargained like this over the content of our interviews. He would tell me something newsworthy and I would ask if I could put that in the newspaper. He would ponder the potential effects and, more often than not, consent. I would then share the nuggets at the office. Sometimes I would direct a reporter to go in the front door and ask Stockman or other officials questions he had already answered through the back door. Sometimes he would bring up matters on his own, items he wanted to see in print. On a few occasions, he absolutely refused to answer my questions because he regarded the information as too sensitive—and too tempting—for me to be trusted with it. From time to time he would complain about some aspects of the *Post's* coverage, particularly the stories which detailed who was going to suffer from the Reagan budget cuts, but he also praised some stories and individual reporters, particularly the ones whose analysis cut through the public rhetoric and described the true core of the policy debates.

Over the months, obviously, this was a useful arrangement for me as an editor at the *Post*. The major turning points, from altering the economic assumptions for the original budget forecasts, to the changing of direction in spring, to the climactic battle over defense spending, were all described in advance in newspaper stories, albeit usually attributed to a "senior budget official" or some other suitable cover. Knowledge of the arrangement and its fruits were discreetly shared among the appropriate editors and reporters at the *Post*. Still, I was surprised to learn afterwards that Stockman himself had apparently boasted to *his* colleagues about the arrangement. After the public controversy, Jude Wanniski, former *Wall Street Journal* editorial writer and an original apostle of supply-side economics, complained bitterly about the relationship in an interview with the *Village Voice:*

> "What has depressed me personally most over the year is the relationship Stockman developed with the *Washington Post*. His position as the Deep Throat . . . with Greider, Bob Kaiser, Caroline Atkinson. The whole *Washington Post* was wired into David Stockman. He would supply them with all the secrets, inner thoughts of the administration, meet with them over and over and over again. It's become the standard practice at the *Post*, to have their Deep Throat and get a Pulitzer Prize. That was the intellectual content of it."
>
> "So this arrangement was all in place back in January, February?"
>
> "Oh, yes. Stockman began telling us when he was part of the group, back in 1979, that he was establishing

a connection with Greider. He announced this to us as a coup. We said that's great. We wanted journalists who were opposed to us to sit down and listen to us, because the whole thing that keeps us moving is our ability to communicate ideas."

I did also say that this arrangement was routine. Notwithstanding Wanniski's melodramatic description, I believe it was. Others in the press make their own transactions in which information is shared for self-interested purposes. Once, for instance, when I came to breakfast, I had to wait my turn because Stockman was finishing breakfast with Robert Novak, who writes the Evans and Novak syndicated political column. On another occasion, my appointment was preceded by one with Joseph Kraft. George Will, we already know, was Stockman's friend and confidant. Nor is this remarkable. Stockman may have been more systematic and bold in his pursuit of linkages with the press, but he was doing what virtually every "senior official" of government does routinely. Partly, I suppose, it is required as self-protection. Largely, I think, it is a discreet form of veiled communication that press and policymakers find useful. It has developed and flourished over many years, a way in which participants in the political debates can argue with each other in semi-public disguises, sending critical messages to colleagues, attacking adversaries, influencing the flow of public dialogue and the content of elite opinion without having to answer directly for their utterances. After a time one develops an insider's skill at reading these veiled messages. As Wanniski suggested, he could study the news columns of the *Post* and conclude that Stockman was the unnamed source. Or a White House official might read an Evans and Novak column and form a reasonable hunch about which anonymous senator was attacking the President. Or the Pentagon might easily discern in a critical "news analysis" piece in the *New York Times* that the Secretary of State or his assistants had provided the ammunition. This coded dialogue may or may not contribute anything of value to the governance of the republic; at the very least it is a closed conversation which only the sophisticated few can follow. Other citizens may be baffled by it, more likely they are bored because it is so opaque.

I assume that David Stockman said much the same thing to other journalists, reporters, and columnists, that he said to me. As an insider who can read the code, I could study the coverage of the *New York Times* and the *Wall Street Journal* and the columnists and see muffled reflections of the same reality that Stockman was describing so vividly in our conversations. Evans and Novak began the year describing Stockman in the most admiring terms; by late summer, when it was clear that Stockman wanted to cut the Pentagon budget, Evans and Novak portrayed him as an enemy. Joseph Kraft, while never citing Stockman as a source, described with remarkable consistency the same story that I eventually told in full. I was struck, in particular, by a Kraft column in early September, two months before the publication of my *Atlantic* piece, which was an uncannily concise outline of the same story I was telling. Kraft observed the same gloomy predicament confronting the Reagan Administration: "A loss of intellectual bearings describes most clearly what has happened." And: "Events have now buried the theory of expectations in the same grave as the view that wishing will make it so. Far from creating confidence and smashing inflation, passage of the President's program fortified the conviction that government deficits will rise." Kraft noted that "some in the administration recognize what is happening." He cited only one example: David Stockman.

This inside knowledge provides a continuing subtext for the news of Washington; very little of it is conveyed in intelligible terms to the uninformed. The "rules" prevent that, and so also do the conventions of the press, how a story is written and what meets the standard definition of what is news. The insiders, both reporters and government officials, will read every news story with this subtext clearly in mind. Other readers are left to struggle with their own translation.

By now, it should be clear why Stockman and I both offended the "rules." The appearance in print of the budget director's candid commentaries shocked sophisticated readers but they were not surprised by the substance of what he was saying. Those who had followed the coded dialogue, who had translated the news stories about "senior budget officials," or perhaps heard Stockman say the same things in private meetings, knew well enough where he stood. Still, it was shocking. The unvarnished private dialogue of government is supposed to remain private— and separate from the bland, reassuring rhetoric of the public discourse. By going public, he violated the privacy and prerogatives of that network and so did I. Publishing the raw version of reality automatically depreciates the value of every insider's knowledge. It also refutes the images of order and progress conveyed by the daily news. These stories of doubt and misgivings and policy battles had, in fact, been printed in the newspapers, but clearly they were not told in a way that made much impression outside the inner circle. As a newspaper editor, thinking my submerged conversations were helping to inform general readers, I was most troubled by my belated recognition that the messages were not getting through.

As a reporter, collecting a rare account of the chaotic realities of government, I felt a different obligation. I wanted to retell Stockman's singular story in a way that would allow the broadest understanding of what had occurred. I knew that many of his offhand remarks would sound sensational, but I wanted to be fair to the context of the material (as well as to Stockman). I wanted intelligent readers to grasp that the famous and powerful people who make government policy live in the same bewildering context of change and uncertainty that confronts all human endeavor. As a newspaper editor, I worked according to the realm of news, its rules and daily limitations. Now, as a writer, I had an opportunity to tell the whole story.

In early August, after the President's tax and budget legislation was enacted, I concluded that the political drama had reached its natural climax and it was now time to write the full narrative account of what Stockman had told me. I proposed this to him and he agreed. There was no discussion of our "ground rules," but throughout our conversations there were many instances that made it clear to me, at least, that Stockman fully expected his words would be quoted directly in the full account. At several points, when he was making sensitive remarks, he reminded me that his comments were for use later, not now. In one instance, when he was commenting critically on a Republican congressional leader, he pointedly advised me that this material would be permanently "off the record," never to be used. Half-seriously, he suggested I turn off the "damned machine." In early September, at our last meeting, I again reminded him that I was preparing to publish the full account of our conversations and again he assented.

Why did Stockman do it? I will not attempt to read his mind. Perhaps he assumed that his provocative statements were already known to the central players of the Reagan Administration and that few would be shocked (we both misjudged this, I think, and reasonable critics might conclude that we were both lost in the warp of inside knowledge). As a reporter, anxious to tell this enormous story, I did not press for reasons. At his White House press conference, Stockman expressed his own puzzlement:

". . . Almost anything other than maybe an indiscreet quotation or expression or metaphor that was contained in that article basically reflects things that I had been saying in our private deliberations as well as in public comments over the last nine months. It was well known, for instance, that I felt some adjustment needed to be made in the defense program—and it was. It was well known I have strongly felt that if we're going to keep the budget on track, we would have to deal with the matter of entitlement and Social Security. It was well known, during the deliberations of the tax bill, that I felt we should stick to our policy-based rate cuts and depreciation reforms and we should do everything possible— given the legislative circumstances and the realities of the moment—to minimize any excess costs of the bill due to ornaments and secondary matters that would not have an economic effect in the sense of promoting the recovery. . . . So I don't think that there is anything in the article that somehow varies with where my position has been."

This was substantially what he had said to me in private a few weeks earlier, when I was arranging for photographs and reminding him that his published remarks were going to stir up a political tempest. As long as the comments were "substantive" as opposed to "ad hominen" personal attacks, Stockman said he was not concerned about the potential impact. "I've been saying those things all over town for months," he said. After the storm broke, he changed his estimate somewhat. The content would cause him considerable political pain, he told me, but the account was "not unfair to me."

Yet the press was as shocked as the partisan politicians. It was as though editors and reporters had no memory of what they themselves had been reporting for months, albeit in the coded dialogue of insiders' stories. Beyond the inner circle, the public was truly shocked by the news bulletins of Stockman's "confessions?" Why had no one told them any of these things? Why had this been kept secret? The boldness of his candor was transformed by the news into something neither of us had anticipated, a bizarre news event like *Man-Bites-Dog*. In this case, it was, *Public Official Says-What-He-Really-Thinks*.

After the controversy subsided, I was left to ponder a different and larger question about the press. If people were so stunned by the narrative reality in "The Education of David Stockman," then what did that tell us about the reality of the "news" conveyed to them each day throughout the year? Following the news carefully every day, reading the code with an insider's eye, I too thought the substantive "news" of the article had already been largely reported. Obviously, I was wrong about that. The sum of the parts was more powerful because it was a comprehensive narrative, not splintered into daily stories. And the tone of private dialogue, presented in the raw without modification, overwhelmed the daily impact of the same messages delivered in code. The press, including myself of course, was usefully serving its smaller audience of the governing elite but not communicating very clearly with the larger public.

Like the political community it covers, the press may be a prisoner of its own conventions, trapped by rules and reflexes which seem useful and necessary to the practitioners but ultimately limit their effectiveness. In that netherworld of continuous private conversations, reporters and columnists are informed how government officials really feel, but the press is obliged to muffle or moderate the messages, to cloak the hard edges of doubt and disagreement with the opaque mantle of anonymity. In sum, the press communicates much less coherently than it thinks it does.

Among editors and reporters, this is an old struggle, an argument that recurs from time to time when some news organization, notably the *Washington Post*, rebels against the rules and refuses to participate in the private dialogue.

Those rebellions have always failed, partly because of competitive pressures. No one wants to be the only "outsider" when the game is getting as much "inside" dope as possible. So it is difficult to imagine how the press might collectively extricate itself from those seductive webs of private conversation, though I think the democratic dialogue would be improved, on balance, if that were to occur. My own perhaps vain belief is that this book will help modestly.

What was the final lesson for government officials and the press? Despite the shock of truth-telling, Stockman did survive in his job. In most respects, events did confirm his judgments. Is it too romantic to believe the other government officials will take similar risks in the future and let their honest thoughts serve as their defense? I am at least certain that other ambitious reporters will seek similar opportunities, soliciting new kinds of arrangements which will allow more of the private reality to reach the larger audience unmuffled. Only in Washington, after all, is it considered bizarre when someone important comes forward and tells the truth. It might also help if the press acts less horrified the next time it happens.

The
Education of
David Stockman

I.
How the World Works

Generally, he had no time for idle sentimentality, but David A. Stockman indulged himself for a moment as he and I approached the farmhouse in western Michigan where Stockman was reared. With feeling, he described a youthful world of hard work, variety, and manageable challenges. "It's something that's disappearing now, the working family farm," Stockman observed. "We had a little of everything—an acre of strawberries, an acre of peaches, a field of corn, fifteen cows. We did everything."

A light snow had fallen the day before, dusting the fields and orchards with white, which softened the dour outline of the Stockman brick farmhouse. It was built seventy years ago by Stockman's maternal grandfather, who also planted the silver birches that ring the house. He was county treasurer of Berrien County for twenty years, and his reputation in local politics was an asset for his grandson.

The farm has changed since Stockman's boyhood; it is more specialized. The bright-red outbuildings behind the house include a wooden barn where livestock was once kept, a chicken coop also no longer in use, a garage, and a large metal-sided building, where the heavy equipment—in particular, a mechanical grape picker—is stored. Grapes are now the principal crop that Allen Stockman, David's father, produces. He earns additional income by leasing out the grape picker. The farm is a small but authentic example of the entrepreneurial capitalism that David Stockman so admires.

As the car approached the house, Stockman's attention was diverted by a minor anomaly in the idyllic rural landscape: two tennis courts. They seemed out of place, alone, amidst the snow-covered fields at an intersection next to the Stockman farm. Stockman hastened to explain that, despite appearances, these were not his family's private tennis courts. They belonged to the township. Royalton Township (of which Al Stockman was treasurer) had received, like all other local units of government, its portion of the federal revenue-sharing funds, and this was how the trustees had decided to spend part of the money from Washington. "It's all right, I suppose," Stockman said amiably, "but these people would never have taxed themselves to build that. Not these tight-fisted taxpayers! As long as someone is giving them the money, sure, they are willing to spend it. But they would never have used their own money."

Stockman's contempt was directed not at the local citizens who had spent the money but at the people in Washington who had sent it. And soon he would be in a position to do something about them. This winter weekend was a final brief holiday with his parents; in a few weeks he would become director of the Office of Management and Budget in the new administration in Washington. Technically, Stockman was still the U. S. congressman from Michigan's Fourth District, but his mind and exceptional energy were already concentrated on running OMB, a small but awesomely complicated power center in the federal government, through which a President attempts to monitor all of the other federal bureaucracies.

Stockman carried with him a big black binder enclosing a "Current Services Budget," which listed every federal program and its current cost projections. He hoped to memorize the names of 500 to 1,000 program titles and major accounts by the time he was sworn in—an objective that seemed reasonable to him, since he already knew many of the budget details. During four years in Congress, Stockman had made himself a leading conservative gadfly, attacking Democratic budgets and proposing leaner alternatives. Now the President-elect was inviting him to do the same thing from within. Stockman had lobbied for the OMB job and was probably better prepared for it, despite his youthfulness, than most of his predecessors.

He was thirty-four years old and looked younger. His shaggy hair was streaked with gray, and yet he seemed like a gawky collegian, with unstylish glasses and a prominent Adam's apple. In the corridors of the Capitol, where all ambitious staff aides scurried about in serious blue suits, Representative Stockman wore the same uniform, and was frequently mistaken for one of them.

Inside the farmhouse, the family greetings were casual and restrained. His parents and his brothers and in-laws did not seem overly impressed by the prospect that the eldest son would soon occupy one of the most powerful positions of government. Opening presents in the cluttered living room, watching the holiday football games on television, the Stockmans seemed a friendly, restrained, classic Protestant farm family of the Middle West, conservative and striving. As sometimes happens in those families, however, the energy and ambition seemed to have been concentrated disproportionately in one child, David, perhaps at the expense of the others. His mother, Carol, a big-boned woman with metallic blond hair, was the family organizer, an active committee member in local Republican politics, and the one who made David work for A's in school. In political debate, David Stockman was capable of dazzling opponents with words; his brothers seemed shy and taciturn in his presence. One brother worked as a county corrections officer in Michigan. Another, after looking on Capitol Hill, found a job in an employment agency. A third, who had that distant look of a sixties child grown older, did day labor, odd jobs. His sister was trained as an educator and worked as a consultant to manpower-training programs in Missouri that were financed by the federal government. "She believes in what she's doing and I don't quarrel with it," Stockman said. "Basically, there are gobs of this money out there. CETA grants have to do evaluation and career planning and so forth. What does it amount to? Somebody rents a room in a Marriott Hotel somewhere and my sister comes in and talks to them. I think Marriott may get more out of it than anyone else. That's part of what we're trying to get at, and it's layered all over the government."

While David Stockman would speak passionately against the government in Washington and its self-aggrandizing habits, there was this small irony about his siblings and himself: most of them worked for government in one way or another—protected from the dynamic risk-taking of the private economy. Stockman himself had never had any employer other than the federal government, but the adventure in his career lay in challenging it. Or, more precisely, in challenging the "permanent government" that modern liberalism had spawned.

By that phrase, Stockman and other conservatives meant not only the layers and layers of federal bureaucrats and liberal politicians who sustained open-ended growth of the central government but also the less visible infrastructure of private interests that fed off of it and prospered—the law firms and lobbyists and trade associations in rows of shining office buildings along K Street in Washington; the consulting firms and contractors; the constituencies of special interests, from schoolteachers to construction workers to failing businesses and multinational giants, all of whom came to Washington for money and for legal protection against the perils of free competition.

While ideology would guide Stockman in his new job, he would be confronted with a large and tangible political problem: how to resolve the three-sided dilemma created by Ronald Reagan's contradictory campaign promises. In private, Stockman agreed that his former congressional mentor, John Anderson, running as an independent candidate for President in 1980, had asked the right question: How is it possible to raise defense spending, cut income taxes, and balance the budget, all at the same time? Anderson had taunted Reagan with that question, again and again, and most conventional political thinkers, from orthodox Republican to Keynesian liberal, agreed with Anderson that it could not be done.

But Stockman was confident, even cocky, that he and some of his fellow conservatives had the answer. It was a theory of economics—the supply-side theory—that promised an end to the twin aggravations of the 1970s: high inflation and stagnant growth in America's productivity. "We've got to figure out a way to make John Anderson's question fit into a plausible policy path over the next three years," Stockman said. "Actually, it isn't all that hard to do."

The supply-side approach, which Stockman had only lately embraced, assumed, first of all, that dramatic action by the new President, especially the commitment to a three-year reduction of the income tax, coupled with tight monetary control, would signal investors that a new era was dawning, that the growth of government would be displaced by the robust growth of the private sector. If economic behavior in a climate of high inflation is primarily based on expectations about the future value of money, then swift and dramatic action by the President could reverse the gloomy assumptions in the disordered financial markets. As inflation abated, interest rates dropped, and productive employment grew, those marketplace developments would, in turn, help Stockman balance the federal budget.

"The whole thing is premised on faith," Stockman explained. "On a belief about how the world works." As he prepared the script in his mind, his natural optimism led to bullish forecasts, which were even more robust than the Reagan Administration's public promises. "The inflation premium melts away like the morning mist," Stockman predicted. "It could be cut in half in a very short period of time if the policy is credible. That sets off adjustments and changes in perception that cascade through the economy. You have a bull market in '81, after April, of historic proportions."

How the world works. It was a favorite phrase of Stockman's, frequently invoked in conversation to indicate a coherent view of things, an ideology that was whole and consistent. Stockman took ideology seriously, and this distinguished him from other bright, ambitious politicians who were content to deal with public questions one at a time, without imposing a consistent philosophical framework upon them.

In 1964, when he went off to Michigan State, having played quarterback in high school and participated in Future Farmers of America, Stockman assumed that he would be a farmer, like his father. His political views were orthodox Republican, derived from his mother, and from his reading of *The Conscience of a Conservative*, by Senator Barry Goldwater. "In my first three months, I went through an absolute clash of cultures," Stockman recalls. "My first professor was an atheist and socialist from Brooklyn, and within three months I think he destroyed everything I believed in, from God to the flag." When the Vietnam War became the focus of campus radicalism, Stockman became a leader, and read Herbert Marcuse, C. Wright Mills, and Paul Goodman's critiques of American society. "I became a radical, not in the hard-core sense but in the more casual sense that nearly everybody was on campus in those days. Naturally, as a good Methodist, I looked for the Methodist youth center, which became the anti-war center, because that was the socially conscious thing to do. I was still enough of a farm boy to believe that revolution was God's work."

After graduation, he enrolled at Harvard Divinity School, thinking he might become a great moral philosopher in the tradition of Christian social activists. (He was perhaps also thinking, like so many other students of the time, that divinity school would extend his deferment from the draft.) At Michigan State, he had dropped the study of agriculture and moved into the humanities. At Harvard, he dropped theology and moved into the social sciences (though he never received training as an economist). "I guess I always had a strong intellectual bent, so I needed a strong theory of how the world worked."

When he found the divinity courses uninspiring, he began taking political science and history—studying under neo-conservatives such as James Q. Wilson, Nathan Glazer, and Daniel Patrick Moynihan—and discovered, he said, "that it was possible to have a sophisticated view of the world without being a Marxist." In a Harvard seminar, he made a connection with John Anderson, who was looking for a bright young idea man to help prepare issues for the House Republican Conference, which Anderson chaired. The Illinois congressman was moving gradually leftward in his views; Stockman was continuing his intellectual search in the opposite direction.

Stockman's congressional district was composed of small towns and countryside, a world that worked quite well without Washington, in his view. After dinner at the farm that day, we took a driving tour of the area. The government's good works were everywhere—a new sewer system in Bridgman, a modern municipal building in Stevensville—

but Stockman belittled them as "pork barrel." Stockman's district was overwhelmingly rural and Republican, but he saw it as a fair representation of America.

Indeed, as a congressman, Stockman himself had worked hard to make certain that his Fourth District constituents exploited the system. His office maintained a computerized alert system for grants and loans from the myriad agencies, to make certain that no opportunities were missed. "I went around and cut all the ribbons and they never knew I voted against the damn programs," he said.

Still, more than most other politicians, Stockman was known for standing by his ideological principles, not undermining them. When Congress voted its bail-out financing to rescue Chrysler from bankruptcy, Stockman was the only Michigan representative to oppose it, even though a large town in his district, St. Joseph, would be hurt. The town's largest employer, St. Joe's Auto Specialties, was a Chrysler supplier, and its factory was laying off workers. Its owners were among Stockman's earliest and largest contributors when he first ran for Congress, in 1976. Still, he opposed the bail-out. "Some of them were a little miffed at me and others applauded. I only had one or two argue strenuously with me. They're probably more derogatory behind my back."

Stockman felt protected from local pressures, in a way that most members of Congress do not—partly by the Republicanism of the district but also by the consistency of his ideology. Since he had a clear, strong view of what government ought and ought not to do, he found it easier to resist claims that seemed illegitimate, no matter who their sponsors might be. "Too many politicians are intimidated by the squeaking wheel, in my judgment. Regardless of their ideological viewpoint, they're able to incorporate the squeaking wheel into their general position. If the proposal is pro-business, they call it conservative. If they're from Nebraska, it's pro-farmer. It's whatever serves the constituencies.''

This was the core of his complaint against the modern liberalism launched by Franklin Roosevelt's New Deal. He did not quarrel with the need for basic social-welfare programs, such as unemployment insurance or Social Security; he agreed that the government must regulate private enterprise to protect general health and safety. But liberal politics in its later stages had lost the ability to judge claims, and so yielded to all of them, Stockman thought, creating what he describes as ''constituency-based choice-making,'' which could no longer address larger national interests, including fiscal control. As Stockman saw it, this process did not ameliorate social inequities; it created new ones by yielding to powerful interest groups at the expense of everyone else. ''What happens is the politicization of the society. All decisions flow to the center. Once we decide to allocate credit to certain activities—and we're doing that on a massive scale—or to allocate the capital for energy development, the levels of competency and morality fall. Then the outcomes in society begin to look more and more like the work of brute muscle. The other thing it does is destroy ideas. Once things are allocated by political muscle, by regional claims, there are no longer idea-based agendas.''

Across the river from St. Joe's, Stockman drove through the deserted Main Street of Benton Harbor, his favorite example of failed liberalism. Once it had been a prosperous commercial center, but now most of its stores and buildings were boarded up and vacant except for an occasional storefront church or social-service agency. As highways and suburban shopping centers pulled away commerce, the downtown collapsed, whites moved, and the city became predominantly black and overwhelmingly poor. The federal government's various efforts to revive Benton Harbor had quite visibly failed.

"When you have powerful underlying demographic and economic forces at work, federal intervention efforts designed to reverse the tide turn out to have rather anemic effects," Stockman said, surveying the dilapidated storefronts. "I wouldn't be surprised if $100 million had been spent here in the last twenty years. Urban renewal, CETA, model cities, they've had everything. And the results? No impact whatever."

The drastic failure seemed to please him, for it confirmed his view of how the world works. As budget director, he intended to proceed against many of the programs that fed money to the poor blacks of Benton Harbor, morally confident because he *knew* from personal observation that the federal revitalization money did not deliver what such programs promised. But he would also go after the Economic Development Administration (EDA) grants for the comfortable towns and the Farmers Home Administration loans for communities that could pay for their own sewers and the subsidized credit for farmers and business—the federal guarantees for economic interests that ought to take their own risks. He was confident of his theory, because, in terms of the Michigan countryside where he grew up, he saw it as equitable and fundamentally moral.

"We are interested in curtailing weak claims rather than weak clients," he promised. "The fear of the liberal remnant is that we will only attack weak clients. We have to show that we are willing to attack powerful clients with weak claims. I think that's critical to our success—both political and economic success."

II.
A Radical in Power

Three weeks before the inauguration, Stockman and his transition team of a dozen or so people were already established at the OMB office in the Old Executive Office Building. When his appointment as budget director first seemed likely, he had agreed to meet with me from time to time and relate, off the record, his private account of the great political struggle ahead. The particulars of these conversations were not to be reported until later, after the season's battles were over, but a cynic familiar with how Washington works would understand that the arrangement had obvious symbiotic value. As an assistant managing editor at the *Washington Post*, I benefited from an informed view of policy discussions of the new administration; Stockman, a student of history, was contributing to history's record and perhaps influencing its conclusions. For him, our meetings were another channel—among many he used—to the press. The older generation of orthodox Republicans distrusted the press; Stockman was one of the younger "new" conservatives who cultivated contacts with columnists and reporters, who saw the news media as another useful tool in political combat. "We believe our ideas have intellectual respectability, and we think the press will recognize that," he said. "The traditional Republicans probably sensed, even

13

if they didn't know it, that their ideas lacked intellectual respectability."

In early January, Stockman and his staff were assembling dozens of position papers on program reductions and studying the internal forecasts for the federal budget and the national economy. The initial figures were frightening—"absolutely shocking," he confided—yet he seemed oddly exhilarated by the bad news, and was bubbling with new plans for coping with these horrendous numbers. A government computer, programmed as a model of the nation's economic behavior, was instructed to estimate the impact of Reagan's program on the federal budget. It predicted that if the new President went ahead with his promised three-year tax reduction and his increase in defense spending, the Reagan Administration would be faced with a series of federal deficits without precedent in peacetime—ranging from $82 billion in 1982 to $116 billion in 1984. Even Stockman blinked. If those were the numbers included in President Reagan's first budget message, the following month, the financial markets that Stockman sought to reassure would instead be panicked. Interest rates, already high, would go higher; the expectation of long-term inflation would be confirmed.

Stockman saw opportunity in these shocking projections. "All the conventional estimates just wind up as mud," he said. "As absurdities. What they basically say, to boil it down, is that the world doesn't work."

Stockman set about doing two things. First, he changed the economic assumptions fed into the computer model. Assisted by like-minded supply-side economists, the new team discarded orthodox premises of how the economy would behave. Instead of a continuing double-digit inflation, they assumed a swift decline in prices and interest rates. Instead of the continuing pattern of slow economic growth, the new model was based on a dramatic surge in the nation's productivity. New investment, new jobs, and growing profits—and Stockman's historic bull market. "It's based on valid economic analysis," he said, "but it's the inverse of the last four years. When we go public, this is going to set off a wide-open debate on how the economy works, a great battle over the conventional theories of economic performance."

The original apostles of supply side, particularly Representative Jack Kemp, of New York, and the economist Arthur B. Laffer, dismissed budget-cutting as inconsequential to the economic problems, but Stockman was trying to fuse new theory and old. "Laffer sold us a bill of goods," he said, then corrected his words: "Laffer wasn't wrong—he didn't go far enough."

The great debate never quite took hold in the dimensions that Stockman had anticipated, but the Reagan Administration's economic projections did become the source of continuing controversy. In defense of their counter-theories, Stockman and his associates would argue, correctly, that conventional forecasts, particularly by the Council of Economic Advisers in the preceding administration, had been consistently wrong in the past. His critics would contend that the supply-side premises were based upon wishful thinking, not sound economic analysis.

But, second, Stockman used the appalling deficit projections as a valuable talking point in the policy discussions that were under way with the President and his principal advisers. Nobody in that group was the least bit hesitant about cutting federal programs, but Reagan had campaigned on the vague and painless theme that eliminating "waste, fraud, and mismanagement" would be sufficient to balance the accounts. Now, as Stockman put it, "the idea is to try to get beyond the waste, fraud, and mismanagement modality and begin to confront the real dimensions of budget reduction." On the first Wednesday in January, Stockman had two hours on the President-elect's schedule to describe the "dire shape" of the federal budget; for starters, the new administration would have to go for a budget reduction in the neighborhood of $40 billion. "Do you have any idea what $40 billion means?" he said. "It means I've got to cut the highway program. It means I've got to cut milk-price supports. And Social Security student benefits. And education and student loans. And manpower training and housing. It means I've got to shut down the synfuels program and a lot of other programs. The idea is to show the magnitude of the budget deficit and some suggestion of the political problems."

How much pain was the new President willing to impose? How many sacred cows would he challenge at once? Stockman was still feeling out the commitment at the White House, aware that Reagan's philosophical commitment to shrinking the federal government would be weighed against political risks.

Stockman was impressed by the ease with which the President-elect accepted the broad objective: find $40 billion in cuts in a federal budget running well beyond $700 billion. But, despite the multitude of expenditures, the proliferation of programs and grants, Stockman knew the exercise was not as easy as it might sound.

Consider the budget in simple terms, as a federal dollar representing the entire $700 billion. The most important function of the federal government is mailing checks to citizens—Social Security checks to the elderly, pension checks to retired soldiers and civil servants, reimbursement checks for hospitals and doctors who provide medical care for the aged and the poor, welfare checks for the dependent, veterans checks to pensioners. Such disbursements consume forty-eight cents of the dollar.

Another twenty-five cents goes to the Pentagon, for national defense. Stockman knew that this share would be rising in the next four years, not shrinking, perhaps becoming as high as thirty cents. Another ten cents was consumed by interest payments on the national debt, which was fast approaching a trillion dollars.

That left seventeen cents for everything else that Washington does. The FBI and the national parks, the county agents and the Foreign Service and the Weather Bureau—all the traditional operations of government—consumed only nine cents of the dollar. The remaining eight cents provided all of the grants to state and local governments, for aiding handicapped children or building highways or installing tennis courts next to Al Stockman's farm. One might denounce particular programs as wasteful, as unnecessary and ineffective, even crazy, but David Stockman knew that he could not escape these basic dimensions of federal spending.

As he and his staff went looking for the $40 billion, they found that most of it would have to be taken from the seventeen cents that covered government operations and grants-in-aid. Defense was already off-limits. Next Ronald Reagan laid down another condition for the budget-cutting: the main benefit programs of Social Security, Medicare, veterans' checks, railroad retirement pensions, welfare for the disabled—the so-called "social safety net" that Reagan had promised not to touch—were to be exempt from the budget cuts. In effect, he was declaring that Stockman could not tamper with three fourths of the forty-eight cents devoted to transfer payments.

No President had balanced the budget in the past twelve years. Still, Stockman thought it could be done, by 1984, if the Reagan Administration adhered to the principle of equity, cutting weak claims, not merely weak clients, and if it shocked the system sufficiently to create a new political climate. He still believed that it was not a question of numbers. "It boils down to a political question, not of budget policy or economic policy, but whether we can change the habits of the political system."

* * *

The struggle began in private, with Ronald Reagan's Cabinet. By inaugural week, Stockman's staff had assembled fifty or sixty policy papers outlining major cuts and alterations, and, aiming at the target of $40 billion, Stockman was anxious to win fast approval for them, before the new Cabinet officers were fully familiar with their departments and prepared to defend their bureaucracies. During that first week, the new Cabinet members had to sit through David Stockman's recital—one proposal after another outlining drastic reductions in their programs. Brief discussion was followed by presidential approval. "I have a little nervousness about the heavy-handedness with which I am being forced to act," Stockman conceded. "It's not that I wouldn't want to give the decision papers to the Cabinet members ahead of time so they could look at them, it's just that we're getting them done at eight o'clock in the morning and rushing them to the Cabinet room . . . It doesn't work when you have to brace these Cabinet officers in front of the President with severe reductions in their agencies, because then they're in the position of having to argue against the group line. And the group line is cut, cut, cut. So that's a very awkward position for them, and you make them resentful very fast."

Stockman proposed to White House counselor Edwin Meese an alternative approach—a budget working group, in which each Cabinet secretary could review the proposed cuts and argue against them. As the group evolved, however, with Meese, chief of staff James Baker, Treasury Secretary Donald Regan, and policy director Martin Anderson, among others, it was stacked in Stockman's favor. "Each meeting will involve only the relevant Cabinet member and his aides with four or five strong keepers of the central agenda," Stockman explained at one point. "So on Monday, when we go into the decision on synfuels programs, it will be [Energy Secretary James B.] Edwards defending them against six guys saying that, by God, we've got to cut these back or we're not going to have a savings program that will add up.''

In general, the system worked. Stockman's agency did in a few weeks what normally consumes months; the process was made easier because the normal opposition forces had no time to marshal either their arguments or their constituents and because the President was fully in tune with Stockman. After the budget working group reached a decision, it would be taken to Reagan in the form of a memorandum, on which he could register his approval by checking a little box. "Once he checks it," Stockman said, "I put that in my safe and I go ahead and I don't let it come back up again."

The check marks were given to changes in twelve major budget entitlements and scores of smaller ones. Eliminate Social Security minimum benefits. Cap the runaway costs of Medicaid. Tighten eligibility for food stamps. Merge the trade adjustment assistance for unemployed industrial workers with standard unemployment compensation and shrink it. Cut education aid by a quarter. Cut grants for the arts and humanities in half. "Zero out" CETA and the Community Services Administration and National Consumer Cooperative Bank. And so forth. "Zero out" became a favorite phrase of Stockman's; it meant closing down a program "cold turkey," in one budget year. Stockman believed that any compromise on a program that ought to be eliminated—funding that would phase it out over several years—was merely a political ruse to keep it alive, so it might still be in existence a few years hence, when a new political climate could allow its restoration to full funding.

"I just wish that there were more hours in the day or that we didn't have to do this so fast. I have these stacks of briefing books and I've got to make decisions about specific options . . . I don't have time, trying to put this whole package together in three weeks, so you just start making snap judgments.''

In the private deliberations, Stockman began to encounter more resistance from Cabinet members. He was proposing to cut $752 million from the Export-Import Bank, which provides subsidized financing for international trade—a cut of crucial symbolic importance, because of Stockman's desire for equity. Two thirds of the Ex-Im's direct loans benefit some of America's major manufacturers—Boeing, Lockheed, General Electric, Westinghouse, McDonnell Douglas, Western Electric, Combustion Engineering—and, not surprisingly, the program had a strong Republican constituency on Capitol Hill. Stockman thought the trade subsidies offended the free-market principles that all conservatives espouse—in particular, President Reagan's objective of withdrawing Washington from business decision-making. Supporters of the subsidies made a practical argument: the U.S. companies, big as they were, needed the financial subsidies to stay even against government-subsidized competition from Europe and Japan.

The counter-offensive against the cut was led by Commerce Secretary Malcolm Baldrige and U. S. Trade Representative William Brock, who argued eloquently before the budget working group for a partial restoration of Ex-Im funds. By Stockman's account, the two ''fought, argued, pounded the table,'' and the meeting seemed headed for deadlock. ''I sort of innocently asked, well, isn't there a terrible political spin on this? It's my impression that most of the money goes to a handful of big corporations, and if we are ever caught not cutting this while we're biting deeply into the social programs, we're going to have big problems.'' Stockman asked if anyone at the table had any relevant data. Deputy Secretary of the Treasury Tim McNamar thereupon produced a list of Ex-Im's major beneficiaries (a list that Stockman had given him before the meeting). "So then I went into this demagogic tirade about how in the world can I cut food stamps and social services and CETA jobs and EDA jobs and you're going to tell me you can't give up one penny for Boeing?"

Stockman won that argument, for the moment. But, as with all the other issues in the budget debate, the argument was only beginning. "I've got to take something out of Boeing's hide to make this look right . . . You can measure me on this, because I'll probably lose but I'll give it a helluva fight."

Stockman also began what was to become a continuing struggle, occasionally nasty, with the new secretary of energy. Edwards, a dentist from South Carolina, was ostensibly appointed to dismantle the Department of Energy, as Reagan had promised, but when Stockman proposed cutting the department in half, virtually eliminating the vast synthetic-fuels program launched by the Carter Administration, Edwards argued in defense. In the midst of the battle, Stockman said contemptuously, "I went over to DOE the other day and here's a whole roomful of the same old bureaucrats I've been kicking around for the last five years—advising Edwards on why we couldn't do certain things on oil decontrol that I wanted to do." The relationship did not improve as the two men got to know each other better.

But Stockman felt only sympathy for Secretary of Agriculture John Block, an Illinois farmer. The budget cuts were hitting some of Agriculture's principal subsidy programs. A billion dollars would be cut from dairy-price supports. The Farmers Home Administration loans and grants were to be sharply curtailed. The low-interest financing for rural electric cooperatives and the Tennessee Valley Authority would be modified. In the early weeks of the new administration, the peanut growers and their congressional lobby had campaigned, as they did every year, to have the new secretary of agriculture raise the price-support level for peanuts. Stockman told Block he would have to refuse—for Stockman wanted to abolish the program. "I sympathize with Jack Block," Stockman said. "I forced him into a position that makes his life miserable over there. He's on the central team, he's not a departmental player, but the parochial politics of that department are fierce." Victories over farm lobbies could be won, Stockman believed, if he kept the issues separate—attacking each commodity program in turn, and undermining urban support by cutting the food and nutrition programs. "My strategy is to come in with a farm bill that's unacceptable to the farm guys so that the whole thing begins to splinter." An early test vote on milk-price supports seemed to confirm the strategy—the dairy farmers lobbied and lost.

The only Cabinet officer Stockman did not challenge was, of course, the secretary of defense. In the frantic preparation of the Reagan budget message, delivered in broad outline to Congress on February 18, the OMB review officers did not give even their usual scrutiny to the new budget projections from Defense. Reagan had promised to increase military spending by 7 percent a year, adjusted for inflation, and this pledge translated into the biggest peacetime arms buildup in the history of the republic—$1.6 trillion over the next five years, which would more than double the Pentagon's annual budget while domestic spending was shrinking. Stockman acknowledged that OMB had taken only a cursory glance at the new defense budget, but he was confident that later on, when things settled down a bit, he could go back and analyze it more carefully.

In late February, months before the defense budget became a subject of Cabinet debate, Stockman privately predicted that Defense Secretary Caspar Weinberger, himself a budget director during the Nixon years, would be an ally when he got around to cutting back military spending. "As soon as we get past this first phase in the process, I'm really going to go after the Pentagon. The whole question is blatant inefficiency, poor deployment of manpower, contracting idiocy, and, hell, I think that Cap's going to be a pretty good mark over there. He's not a tool of the military-industrial complex. I mean, he hasn't been steeped in its excuses and rationalizations and ideology for twenty years, and I think that he'll back off on a lot of this stuff, but you just can't challenge him head-on without your facts in line. And we're going to get our case in line and just force it through the presses.''

Stockman shared the general view of the Reagan Administration that the United States needed a major buildup of its armed forces. But he also recognized that the Pentagon, as sole customer for weapons systems, subsidized the arms manufacturers in many direct ways and violated many free-market principles. "The defense budgets in the out-years won't be nearly as high as we are showing now, in my judgment. Hell, I think there's a kind of swamp of $10 to $20 to $30 billion worth of waste that can be ferreted out if you really push hard.''

Long before President Reagan's speech to Congress, most of the painful details of the $41.4 billion in proposed reductions were already known to Capitol Hill and the public. In early February, preparing the political ground, Stockman started delivering his "black book" to Republican leaders and committee chairmen. He knew that once the information was circulating on the Hill, it would soon be available to the news media, and he was not at all upset by the daily storm of headlines revealing the dimensions of what lay ahead. The news conveyed, in its drama and quantity of detail, the appropriate political message: President Reagan would not be proposing business as usual. The President had in mind what Stockman saw as "fiscal revolution.''

But it was not generally understood that the new budget director had already lost a major component of his revolution—another set of proposals, which he called "Chapter II," that was not sent to Capitol Hill because the President had vetoed its most controversial elements.

Stockman had thought "Chapter II" would help him on two fronts: it would provide substantially increased revenues and thus help reduce the huge deficits of the next three years; but it would also mollify liberal critics complaining about the cuts in social welfare, because it was aimed primarily at tax expenditures (popularly known as "loopholes") benefiting oil and other business interests. "We have a gap which we couldn't fill even with all these budget cuts, too big a deficit," Stockman explained. "Chapter II comes out totally on the opposite of the equity question. That was part of my strategy to force acquiescence at the last minute into a lot of things you'd never see a Republican administration propose. I had a meeting this morning at the White House. The President wasn't involved, but all the other key senior people were. We brought a program of additional tax savings that don't touch any social programs. But they touch tax expenditures." Stockman hesitated to discuss details, for the package was politically sensitive, but it included elimination of the oil-depletion allowance; an attack on tax-exempt industrial-development bonds; user fees for owners of private airplanes and barges; a potential ceiling on home-mortgage deductions (which Stockman called a "mansion cap," since it would affect only the wealthy); some defense reductions; and other items, ten in all. Total additional savings: somewhere in the neighborhood of $20 billion. Stockman was proud of "Chapter II" and also very nervous about it, because, while liberal Democrats might applaud the closing of "loopholes" that they had attacked for years, powerful lobbies—in Congress and business—would mobilize against it.

Did President Reagan approve? "If there's a consensus on it, he's not going to buck it, probably."

Two weeks later, Stockman cheerfully explained that the President had rejected his "tax-expenditures" savings. The "Chapter II" issues had seemed crucial to Stockman when he was preparing them, but he dismissed them as inconsequential now that he had lost. "Those were more like ornaments I was thinking of on the tax side," he insisted. "I call them equity ornaments. They're not really too good. They're not essential to the economics of the thing."

The President was willing to propose user fees for aircraft, private boats, and barges, but turned down the proposal to eliminate the oil-depletion allowance. "The President has a very clear philosophy," Stockman explained. "A lot of people criticize him for being short on the details, but he knows when something's wrong. He just jumped all over my tax proposals."

Stockman dropped other proposals. Nevertheless, he was buoyant. The reactions from Capitol Hill were clamorous, as expected, but the budget director was more impressed by the silences, the stutter and hesitation of the myriad interest groups. Stockman was becoming a favorite caricature for newspaper cartoonists—the grim reaper of the Reagan Administration, the Republican Robespierre—but in his many sessions on the Hill he sensed confusion and caution on the other side.

"There are more and more guys coming around to our side," he reported. "What's happening is that the plan is so sweeping and it covers all the bases sufficiently, so that it's like a magnifying glass that reveals everybody's pores . . . In the past, people could easily get votes for their projects or their interests by saying, well, if they would cut food stamps and CETA jobs and two or three other things, then maybe we would go along with it, but they are just picking on my program. But, now, everybody perceives that everybody's sacred cows are being cut. If that's what it takes, so be it. The parochial player will not be the norm, I think. For a while."

III.

The Magic Asterisk

On Capitol Hill, ideological consistency is not a highly ranked virtue but its absence is useful grounds for scolding the opposition. David Stockman endured considerable needling when his budget appeared, revealing that many programs that he had opposed as a congressman had survived. The most glaring was the fast-breeder nuclear reactor at Clinch River, Tennessee. Why hadn't Stockman cut the nuclear subsidy that he had so long criticized? The answer was Senator Howard Baker, of Tennessee, majority leader. "I didn't have to get rolled," Stockman said, "I just got out of the way. It just wasn't worth fighting. This package will go nowhere without Baker, and Clinch River is just life or death to Baker. A very poor reason, I know."

Consistency, he knew, was an important asset in the new environment. The package of budget cuts would be swiftly picked apart if members of Congress perceived that they could save their pet programs, one by one, from the general reductions. "All those guys are looking for ways out," he said. "If they can detect an alleged pattern of preferential treatment for somebody else or discriminatory treatment between rural and urban interests or between farm interests and industrial interests, they can concoct a case for theirs."

Even by Washington standards, where overachieving

young people with excessive adrenalin are commonplace, Stockman was busy. Back and forth, back and forth he went, from his vast office at the Old Executive Office Building, with its classic high ceilings and its fireplace, to the cloakrooms and hideaway offices and hearing chambers of the Capitol, to the West Wing of the White House. Usually, he carried an impossible stack of books and papers under his arm, like a harried high school student who has not been given a locker. He promised friends he would relax—take a day off, or at least sleep later than 5 A.M., when he usually arose to read policy papers before breakfast. But he did not relax easily. What was social life compared with the thrill of reshaping the federal establishment?

In the early skirmishing on Capitol Hill, Stockman actually proposed a tight control system: Senator Baker and the House Republican leader, Robert Michel, of Illinois, would be empowered to clear all budget trades on particular programs—and no one else, not even the highest White House advisers, could negotiate any deals. "If you have multiple channels for deals to be cut and retreats to be made," Stockman explained, "then it will be possible for everybody to start side-dooring me, going in to see Meese, who doesn't understand the policy background, and making the case, or [James] Baker making a deal with a subcommittee chairman." Neither the White House nor the congressional leadership liked his idea, and it was soon buried.

By March, however, Stockman could see the status quo yielding to the shock of the Reagan agenda. In dozens of meetings and hearings, public and private, Stockman perceived that it was now inappropriate for a senator or a congressman to plead for his special interests, at least in front of other members with other interests. At one caucus, a Tennessee Republican began to lecture him on the reduced financing for TVA; other Republicans scolded him.

Stockman cut public-works funding for the Red River project in Louisiana, which he knew would arouse Russell Long, former chairman of the Senate Finance Committee. Long appealed personally at the White House, and Reagan stood firm.

One by one, small signals such as these began to change Stockman's estimate of the political struggle. He began to believe that the Reagan budget package, despite its scale, perhaps because of its scale, could survive in Congress. With skillful tactics by political managers, with appropriate public drama provided by the President, the relentless growth rate of the federal budget, a permanent reality of Washington for twenty years, could actually be contained.

Stockman's analysis was borne out a few weeks later, in early April, when the Senate adopted its first budget-cutting measures, 88-10, a package close enough to the administration's proposals to convince Stockman of the vulnerability of "constituency-based" politics. "That could well be a turning point in this whole process," Stockman said afterward.

Still, Stockman was even more impressed by the performance of the new Republican majority in the Senate. After a week of voting down amendments to restore funds for various programs—"voting against every motherhood title," as Stockman put it—moderate Republicans from the Northeast and Midwest needed some sort of political solace. Led by Senator John Chaffee, of Rhode Island, the moderates proposed an amendment spreading about $1 billion over an array of social programs, from education to home-heating assistance for the poor. Stockman had no objection. The amendment wouldn't cost much overall, and it would "take care of those people who have been good soldiers." Senator Pete Domenici, of New Mexico, the Senate budget chairman, decided, however, that the accommodation wasn't necessary, and he was right. The Chaffee amendment lost.

"It was the kind of amendment that should have passed," Stockman reflected afterward. "The fact that it didn't win tells me that the political logic has changed."

Not entirely, however. While the Senate majority was rejecting additional money for the coalition of social programs, it was also tinkering with an important item in Stockman's balance of equitable cuts—the Export-Import Bank. The great multinational industrial firms that received the trade subsidies from Ex-Im were already at work, arguing that U.S. sales abroad and jobs at home would suffer without the Ex-Im loans and guarantees. The Republicans, led by Senator Nancy Kassebaum, of Kansas, where Boeing is a major employer, voted to restore $250 million to the Ex-Im budget. Later, the House raised the figure even higher, with little resistance from the White House.

"We weren't really closely in control," Stockman explained. "The mark-up went so fast, and those amendments came out of the woodwork, and we weren't prepared to deal with it." Stockman seemed nonchalant about his defeat. The principle of cutting the Ex-Im's corporate subsidies, which had seemed so important to him in January, was now regarded as a minor blemish on the Senate victory. "It did open a little breach that is troublesome," he conceded.

The vulnerability of Stockman's ideology was always that the politics of winning would overwhelm the philosophical premises. But after the Senate victory, Stockman devoted his energy to the tactical questions—winning again in the House of Representatives, which was controlled by the Democrats. "This is pure politics," he said. "It's a question of whether the President can prevail on the floor of the House, because if he can't, then the committee chairmen know they have license to do anything they want."

Stockman watched with admiration as his principal in-

tellectual rival, Jim Jones, the Democratic chairman of the
House Budget Committee, attempted to fashion a budget
resolution that would hold the Democratic majority together. The budget director calculated that Jones had an
impossible task, but he could see that the Oklahoma congressman was going to come closer than he had expected.
The Democrats, by Stockman's analysis, were really three
groups: the old-line liberal faithful, who would follow the
party leadership and defend against any or all budget cuts;
a middle group, including Jones and other younger members, who recognized that federal deficits were out of
control and were willing to confront the problem (Stockman referred to them as "the progressives"); and, finally,
the "boll weevils," the thirty-eight southerners who were
pulled toward Reagan both in conservative philosophy and
by the politics of their home districts, which had voted
overwhelmingly for the President. Jones was drawing up a
resolution that would restore some funds to social programs, to keep the liberals happy; that projected a smaller
deficit than Stockman's, to appear more responsible in
fiscal terms; and that did not touch the defense budget,
which would offend the southerners.

Artful as it was, the Jones resolution was, according to
Stockman, a series of gimmicks: economic estimates and
accounting tricks. "Political numbers," he called them.
But Stockman was not critical of Jones for these budget
ploys, because he cheerfully conceded that the administration's own budget numbers were constructed on similar
shaky premises, mixing cuts from the original 1981 budget
left by Jimmy Carter with new baseline projections from
the Congressional Budget Office in a way that, fundamentally, did not add up. The budget politics of 1981, which
produced such clear and dramatic rhetoric from both sides,
was, in fact, based upon a bewildering set of numbers that
confused even those, like Stockman, who produced them.

"None of us really understands what's going on with all

these numbers," Stockman confessed at one point. "You've got so many different budgets out and so many different baselines and such complexity now in the interactive parts of the budget between policy action and the economic environment and all the internal mysteries of the budget, and there are a lot of them. People are getting from A to B and it's not clear how they are getting there. It's not clear how we got there, and it's not clear how Jones is going to get there."

These "internal mysteries" of the budget process were not dwelt upon by either side, for there was no point in confusing the clear lines of political debate with a much deeper and unanswerable question: Does anyone truly understand, much less control, the dynamics of the federal budget intertwined with the mysteries of the national economy? Stockman pondered this question occasionally, but since there was no obvious remedy, no intellectual construct available that would make sense of this anarchical universe, he was compelled to shrug at the mystery and move ahead. "I'm beginning to believe that history is a lot shakier than I ever thought it was," he said, in a reflective moment. "In other words, I think there are more random elements, less determinism and more discretion, in the course of history than I ever believed before. Because I can see it."

The "random elements" were working in Stockman's behalf in the House of Representatives. He had a good fix on what Jones would produce as the Democratic alternative, in part because he had a spy in the Democratic meetings—Phil Gramm, of Texas, a like-minded conservative and friend who agreed to co-sponsor the administration's substitute resolution. Did Jones know that one of his Democratic committee members was really on the other side? "No," said Stockman. "That's how I know what's in Jones's budget."

Stockman was also dealing with the recognized leaders

of the "boll weevils." He thought that the southerners could be won to the President's side with a minimum of trading, but he was prepared to trade. He agreed with G. V. "Sonny" Montgomery, chairman of the House Veterans' Affairs Committee and a genuine leader among the southern Democrats, to acquiesce in the restoration of $350 to $400 million for staffing at veterans' hospitals. Once Montgomery announced he was with the President, it would be a respectable position, which other southerners could embrace, Stockman felt. Still, he was confident that he could defend the agenda against general trading for votes.

In political terms, Stockman's analysis was sound. The Reagan program was moving toward a series of dramatic victories in Congress. Beyond the brilliant tactical maneuvering, however, and concealed by the public victories, Stockman was privately staring at another reality—a gloomy portent that the economic theory behind the President's program wasn't working. While it was winning in the political arena, the plan was losing on Wall Street. The financial markets, which Stockman had thought would be reassured by the new President's bold actions, and which were supposed to launch a historic "bull market" in April, failed to respond in accordance with Stockman's script. The markets not only failed to rally, they went into a new decline. Interest rates started up again; the bond market slumped. The annual inflation rate, it was true, was declining, dropping below double digits, but even Stockman acknowledged that this was owing to "good luck" with grain harvests and world oil supplies, not to Reaganomics. Investment analysts, however, were looking closely at the Stockman budget figures, looking beyond the storm of political debate and the President's winning style, and what they saw were enormous deficits ahead—the same numbers that had shocked David Stockman when he came into office in January. Henry Kaufman, of Salomon Brothers, one of the preeminent prophets of Wall Street, delivered a sobering speech that, in the cautious language of financiers, said the same thing that John Anderson had said in 1980: cutting taxes and pumping up the defense budget would produce not balanced budgets but inflationary deficits.

Was Kaufman right? Stockman agreed that he was, and conceded that his own original conception—that dramatic political action would somehow alter the marketplace expectations of continuing inflation—had been wrong. "They're concerned about the out-year budget posture, not about the near-term economic situation. The Kaufmans don't dispute our diagnosis at all. They dispute our remedy. They don't think it adds up . . . I take the performance of the bond market deadly seriously. I think it's the best measure there is. The bond markets represent worldwide psychology, worldwide perception and evaluation of what, on balance, relevant people think about what we're doing . . . It means we're going to have to make changes . . . I wouldn't say we are losing. We're still not winning. We're not winning."

The underlying problem of the deficits first surfaced, to Stockman's embarrassment, in the Senate Budget Committee in mid-April, when committee Republicans choked on the three-year projections supplied by the nonpartisan Congressional Budget Office. Three Republican senators refused to vote for a long-term budget measure that predicted continuing deficits of $60 billion, instead of a balanced budget by 1984.

Stockman thought he had taken care of embarrassing questions about future deficits with a device he referred to as the "magic asterisk." (Senator Howard Baker had dubbed it that in strategy sessions, Stockman said.) The "magic asterisk" would blithely denote all of the future deficit problems that were to be taken care of with additional budget reductions, to be announced by the President at a later date. Thus, everyone could finesse the hard questions, for now.

But, somehow or other, the Senate Budget Committee staff insisted upon putting the honest numbers in its resolution—the projected deficits of $60 billion-plus running through 1984. That left the Republican senators staring directly at the same scary numbers that Stockman and the Wall Street analysts had already seen. The budget director blamed this brief flare-up on the frantic nature of his schedule. When he should have been holding hands with the Senate Budget Committee, he was at the other end of the Capitol, soothing Representative Delbert Latta, of Ohio, the ranking Republican in budget matters, who was pouting. Latta thought that since he was a Republican, his name should go ahead of that of Phil Gramm, a Democrat, on the budget resolution: that it should be Latta-Gramm instead of Gramm-Latta.

After a few days of reassurances, Stockman persuaded the Republican senators to relax about the future and two weeks later they passed the resolution—without being given any concrete answers as to where he would find future cuts of such magnitude. In effect, the "magic asterisk" sufficed.

But the real problem, as Stockman conceded, was still unsolved. Indeed, pondering the reactions of financial markets, the budget director made an extraordinary confession in private: the original agenda of budget reductions, which had seemed so radical in February, was exposed by May as inadequate. The "magic asterisk" might suffice for the political debate in Congress, but it would not answer the fundamental question asked by Wall Street: How, in fact, did Ronald Reagan expect to balance the federal budget? "It's a tentative judgment on the part of the markets and of spokesmen like Kaufman that is reversible because they haven't seen all our cards. From the cards they've seen, I suppose that you can see how they draw that conclusion."

"It means," Stockman said, "that you have to have some recalibration in the policy. The thing was put together so fast that it probably should have been put together differently." With mild regret, Stockman looked back at what had gone wrong:

"The defense numbers got out of control and we were doing that whole budget-cutting exercise so frenetically. In other words, you were juggling details, pushing people, and going from one session to another, trying to cut housing programs here and rural electric there, and we were doing it so fast, we didn't know where we were ending up for sure . . . In other words, we should have designed those pieces to be more compatible. But the pieces were moving on independent tracks—the tax program, where we were going on spending, and the defense program, which was just a bunch of numbers written on a piece of paper. And it didn't quite mesh. That's what happened. But, you see, for about a month and a half we got away with that because of the novelty of all these budget reductions."

Reagan's policymakers knew that their plan was wrong, or at least inadequate to its promised effects, but the President went ahead and conveyed the opposite impression to the American public. With the cool sincerity of an experienced television actor, Reagan appeared on network TV to rally the nation in support of the Gramm-Latta resolution, promising a new era of fiscal control and balanced budgets, when Stockman knew they still had not found the solution. This practice of offering the public eloquent reassurances despite privately held doubts was not new, of course. Every contemporary President—starting with Lyndon Johnson, in his attempt to cover up the true cost of the war in Vietnam—had been caught, sooner or later, in contradictions between promises and economic realities. The legacy was a deep popular skepticism about anything a President promised about the economy. Barely four months in office, Ronald Reagan was already adding to the legacy.

Indeed, Stockman began in May to plot what he called the "recalibration" of Reagan policy, which he hoped could be executed discreetly over the coming months to eliminate the out-year deficits for 1983 and 1984 that alarmed Wall Street—without alarming political Washington and losing control in the congressional arena. "It's very tough, because you don't want to end up like Carter, where you put a plan out there and then, a month into it, you visibly and unmistakably change postures. So what you have to do is solve this problem incrementally, without the appearance of reversal, and there are some ways to do that."

Stockman saw three main areas of opportunity for closing the gap: defense, Social Security, and health costs, meaning Medicare and Medicaid. And there was a fourth: the Reagan tax cut; if it could be modified in the course of the congressional negotiations already under way, this would make for additional savings on the revenue side. The public alarm over the deficits was, to some extent, "fortuitous," from Stockman's viewpoint, because the Wall Street message supported the sermon that he was delivering to his fellow policymakers at the White House: the agonies of budget reduction were only beginning, and, more to the point, the Reagan Administration could not keep its promise of balanced budgets unless it was willing to back away from its promised defense spending, its 10-10-10 tax-cut plan, and the President's pledge to exempt from cutbacks the so-called "safety-net" programs. Stockman would deliver this speech, in different forms, all through the summer ahead, trying to create the leverage for action on those fronts, particularly on defense. He later explained his strategy:

"I put together a list of twenty social programs that have to be zeroed out completely, like Job Corps, Head Start, women and children's feeding programs, on and on. And another twenty-five that have to be cut by 50 percent: general revenue sharing, CETA manpower training, etcetera, etcetera. And then huge bites that would have to be taken out of Social Security. I mean really fierce, blood-and-guts stuff—widows' benefits and orphans' benefits, things like that. And still it didn't add up to $40 billion. So that sort of created a new awareness of the defense budget . . .

"Once you set aside defense and Social Security, the Medicare complex, and a few other sacred cows of minor dimension, like the VA and the FBI, you have less than $200 billion worth of discretionary room—only $144 billion after you cut all the easy discretionary programs this year."

In short, the fundamental arithmetic of the federal budget, which Stockman and others had brushed aside in the heady days of January, was now back to haunt them. If the new administration would not cut defense or Social Security or major "safety-net" programs that Reagan had put off limits, then it must savage the smaller slice remaining. Otherwise, balancing the budget in 1984 became an empty promise. The political pain of taking virtually all of the budget savings from government grants and operations would be too great, Stockman believed; Congress would never stand for it. Therefore, he had to begin educating "the West Wing guys" on the necessity for major revisions in their basic plan. He was surprisingly optimistic. "They are now understanding all those things," Stockman said. "A month ago, they didn't. They really thought you could find $144 billion worth of waste, fraud, and abuse. So at least I've made a lot of headway internally."

Revisions of the original tax-cut plan would probably be the easiest compromise. A modest delay in the effective date would save billions and, besides, many conservatives in Congress were never enthusiastic about the supply-side tax-cutting formula. In order to win its passage, the administration was "prepared to give a little bit on the tax bill," Stockman said, which would help cure his problem of deficits.

Social Security was much more volatile, but Stockman noted that the Senate had already expressed a willingness in test votes to reconsider such basic components as annual cost-of-living increases for retirees. In the House, the Democrats, led by J. J. Pickle, of Texas, were preparing their own set of reforms to keep the system from bankruptcy, so Stockman thought it would be possible to develop a consensus for real changes. He didn't much care for Pickle's proposals, because the impact of the reforms stretched out over some years, whereas Stockman was looking for immediate relief. "I'm just not going to spend a lot of political capital solving some other guy's problem in 2010." But he felt sure a compromise could be worked out. "If you don't do this in 1981, this system is going to land on the rocks," he predicted, "because you won't do it in '82 [a congressional election year] and by '83, you will have solvency problems coming out of your ears. You know, sometimes sheer reality has a sobering effect."

Finally, there was defense. Stockman thought the sobering effects of reality were working in his favor there, too, but he recognized that the political tactics were much trickier. In order to get the first round of budget cuts through Congress, particularly in order to lure the southern Democrats to the President's side, there must be no hint of retreat from Reagan's promises for the Pentagon. That would mobilize the defense lobby against him and help the Democrats hold control of the House. Still, when the timing was right, Stockman thought he would prevail.

"They got a blank check," Stockman admitted. "We didn't have time during that February-March period to do anything with defense. Where are we going to cut? Domestic? Or struggle all day and night with defense? So I let it go. But it worked perfectly, because they got so goddamned greedy that they got themselves strung way out there on a limb.''

As policymakers and politicians faced up to the additional cuts required in programs, the pressure would lead them back, inevitably, to a tough-minded re-examination of the defense side. Or so Stockman believed. That combination of events, he suggested, would complete the circle for Wall Street.

''The markets will respond to that. Unless they are absolutely perverse.''

IV.
Old Politics

The President's televised address, in April, was masterly and effective: the nation responded with a deluge of mail and telephone calls, and the House of Representatives accepted Reagan's version of budget reconciliation over the Democratic alternative. The final roll call on the Gramm-Latta resolution was not even close, with sixty-three Democrats joining all House Republicans in support of the President. The stunning victory and the disorganized opposition from the Democrats confirmed for Stockman a political hunch he had first developed when he saw the outlines of Representative Jim Jones's resolution, mimicking the administration's budget-cutting. The 1980 election results may not have been "ideological," but the members of Congress seemed to be interpreting them that way.

This new context, Stockman felt, would be invaluable for the weeks ahead, as the budget-and-tax issues moved into the more complicated and vulnerable areas of action. The generalized budget-cutting instructions voted by the House were now sent to each of the authorizing committees, most of them chaired by old-line liberal Democrats who would try to save the programs in their jurisdictions, but their ability to counterattack was clearly limited by the knowledge that President Reagan, not Speaker Tip O'Neill, controlled the floor of the House. Stockman expected the

Democratic chairmen to employ all of their best legislative tricks to feign cooperation while actually undermining the Reagan budget cuts, but he was already preparing another Republican resolution, dubbed "Son of Gramm-Latta," to make sure the substantive differences were maintained— the block grants that melded social programs and turned them over to the states, the "caps" on Medicaid and other open-ended entitlement programs, the "zeroing out" of others.

In the first round, Stockman felt that he had retreated on very little. He made the trade with Representative Montgomery on VA hospitals, and his old friend Representative Gramm had restored some "phase-out" funds for EDA, the agency Stockman so much wished to abolish. "He put it in there over my objections," Stockman explained, "because he needed to keep three or four people happy. I said okay, but we're not bound by it." The Republican resolution also projected a lower deficit than Stockman thought was realistic, as a tactical necessity. "Gramm felt he couldn't win on the floor unless they had a lower deficit, closer to Jones's deficit, so they got it down to $31 billion by hook or by crook, mostly the latter."

Stockman was supremely confident at that point. The Reagan Administration had taken the measure of its political opposition and had created a new climate in Washington, a new agenda. Now what remained was to follow through in a systematic way that would convince the financial markets. In the middle of May, he made another prediction: the bull market on Wall Street, the one he had expected in April, would arrive by late summer or early fall.

"I think we're on the verge of the response in the financial markets. It takes one more piece of the puzzle, resolution of the tax bill. And that may happen relatively quickly and when it does, I think you'll start a long bull market, by the end of the summer and early fall. The reinforcement that the President got politically in the legislative process will be doubled, barring some new war in the Middle East, by a perceived economic situation in which things are visibly improving. I'm much more confident now.''

Stockman was wrong, of course, about the bull market. But his misinterpretation of events was more profound than that. Without recognizing it at the time, the budget director was headed into a summer in which not only financial markets but life itself seemed to be absolutely perverse. The Reagan program kept winning in public, a series of well-celebrated political victories in Congress—yet privately Stockman was losing his struggle.

Stockman was changing, in a manner that perhaps he himself did not recognize. His conversations began to reflect a new sense of fatalism, a brittle edge of uncertainty.

''There was a certain dimension of our theory that was unrealistic . . .''

''The system has an enormous amount of inertia . . .''

''I don't believe too much in the momentum theory any more . . .''

''I have a new theory—there are no *real* conservatives in Congress . . .''

The turning point, which Stockman did not grasp at the time, came in May, shortly after the first House victory. Buoyed by the momentum, the White House put forward, with inadequate political soundings, the Stockman plan for Social Security reform. Among other things, it proposed a drastic reduction in the benefits for early retirement at age sixty-two. Stockman thought this was a privilege that older citizens could comfortably yield, but 64 percent of those eligible for Social Security were now taking early retirement, and the ''reform'' plan set off a sudden tempest on Capitol Hill. Democrats accused Reagan of reneging on his promise to exempt Social Security from the budget cuts and accused Stockman of trying to balance his budget at the expense of Social Security recipients, which, of course, he was. "The Social Security problem is not simply one of satisfying actuaries," Stockman conceded. "It's one of satisfying the here-and-now of budget requirements." In the initial flurry of reaction, the Senate passed a unanimous resolution opposing the OMB version of how to reform Social Security, and across the nation, the elderly were alarmed enough to begin writing and calling their representatives in Congress. But Stockman seemed not to grasp the depth of his political problem; he still believed that congressional reaction would quiet down eventually and Democrats would cooperate with him.

"Three things," he explained. "First, the politicians in the White House are over-reacting. They're overly alarmed. Second, there is a serious political problem with it, but not of insurmountable dimensions. And third, basically I screwed up quite a bit on the way the damn thing was handled."

Stockman said that Republicans on Ways and Means were urging him to propose an administration reform plan as an alternative to the Democrats'; Stockman misjudged the political climate. The White House plan, put together in haste, had "a lot of technical bloopers," which made it even more vulnerable to attack, Stockman said. "I was just racing against the clock. All the office things I knew ought to be done by way of groundwork, advance preparation, and so forth just fell by the wayside . . . Now we're taking the flak from all the rest of the Republicans because we didn't inform them."

Despite the political uproar, Stockman thought a compromise would eventually emerge, because of the pressure to "save" Social Security. This would give him at least a portion of the budget savings he needed. "I still think we'll recover a good deal of ground from this. It will permit the politicians to make it look like they're doing something *for* the beneficiary population when they are doing something *to* it which they normally wouldn't have the courage to undertake.''

But there was less ''courage'' among politicians than Stockman assumed. Indeed, one politician who scurried away from the President's proposed cuts in Social Security was the President. Stockman wanted him to go on television again, address the nation on Social Security's impending bankruptcy, and build a popular constituency for the changes. But White House advisers did not.

''The President was very interested [in the reform package] and he believed it was the right thing to do. The problem is that the politicians are so wary of the Social Security issue per se that they want to keep him away from it, thinking they could somehow have an administration initiative that came out of the boondocks somewhere and the President wouldn't be tagged with it. Well, that was just pure naive nonsense . . . My view was, if you had to play this thing over, you should have the President go on TV and give a twenty-minute Fireside Chat, with some nice charts . . . You could have created a climate in which major things could be changed.''

The White House rejected that idea. Ronald Reagan kept his distance from the controversy, but it would not go away. In September, Reagan did finally address the issue in a televised chat with the nation: he disowned Stockman's reform plan. Reagan said that there was a lot of ''misinformation'' about in the land, to the effect that the President wanted to cut Social Security. Not true, he declared, though Reagan had proposed such a cut in May. Indeed, the President not only buried the Social Security cuts he had proposed earlier but retreated on one reform measure—elimination of the minimum benefits—that Congress had already, reluctantly, approved. As though he had missed the long debate on that issue, Reagan announced that it was never his intention to deprive anyone who was in genuine need. Any legislative action toward altering

Social Security would be postponed until 1983, after the 1982 congressional elections, and too late to help Stockman with his stubborn deficits. In the meantime, Reagan accepted a temporary solution advocated by the Democrats and denounced by Stockman as "irresponsible"—borrowing from another federal trust fund that was in surplus, the health-care fund, to cover Social Security's problems. Everyone put the best face on it, including Stockman. The tactical retreat, they explained, was the only thing Reagan could do under the circumstances—a smart move, given the explosive nature of the Social Security protest. Still, it was a retreat, and, for David Stockman, a fundamental defeat. He lost one major source of potential budget savings. The political outcome did not suggest that he would do much better when he proposed reforms for Medicare, Social Security's twin.

Where would Stockman find the money to cover those deficits, variously estimated at $44 to $65 billion? The tax-cut legislation itself became one of Stockman's best hopes. The tax bargaining had begun in the spring as a delicate process of private negotiations and reassurances with different groups—with Democrats needed for a House majority, with nervous Republicans still leery of the supply-side theology, and with the supply-side apostles zealously defending their creed. Stockman was a participant, though not the lead player, in this process; he met almost daily with the legislative tactical group at the White House— Edwin Meese, Jim Baker, Donald Regan, presidential assistant Richard Darman, and others—that called signals on both the tax legislation and budget reconciliation.

Stockman's interest was made clear to the others: he wanted a compromise on the tax bill which would substantially reduce its drain on the federal treasury and thus moderate the fiscal damage of Reaganomics. Stockman thought that if the Republicans could compromise with the

Ways and Means chairman, Representative Dan Rostenkowski, the tax legislation would still be a supply-side tax-cut in its approach but considerably smaller in size. More important, they would avoid a bidding war for votes. "We're kind of divided, not in an antagonistic sense, just sort of a judgment sense, between those who want to call off the game . . . and those of us who want to give Rostenkowski a few more days to see what he can achieve."

The negotiations with Rostenkowski ended in failure, and the Reagan team agreed that it would have to modify its own tax-cut plan in order to lure fiscal conservatives. Under the revised plan, the first-year reduction was only 5 percent and, more important, the impact was delayed until late in the year, substantially reducing the revenue loss. The White House also made substantial changes in the business-depreciation and tax-credit rules, which were intended to stimulate new industrial investments, reducing the overly generous provisions for business tax write-offs on new equipment and buildings.

Stockman was privately delighted: he saw a three-year revenue savings of $70 billion in the compromise. The depreciation rules that big business wanted were "way out of joint," Stockman insisted. But he was nervous about the $70 billion figure, because he feared that when Representative Jack Kemp (co-sponsor of the original supply-side tax proposal, the Kemp-Roth bill) and other supply-side advocates heard it, they might regard the savings as so large that it would undermine the stimulative effects of the major tax reduction. "As long as Jack is happy with what's happening," Stockman said, "it's hard for the [supply-side] network to mobilize itself with a shrill voice. Jack's satisfied, although we're sort of on the edge of thin ice with him."

The supply-side effects would still be strong, Stockman said, but he added a significant disclaimer that would have offended true believers, for it sounded like old orthodoxy:

"I've never believed that just cutting taxes alone will cause output and employment to expand."

Stockman himself had been a late convert to supply-side theology, and now he was beginning to leave the church. The theory of "expectations" wasn't working. He could see that. And Stockman's institutional role as budget director forced him to look constantly at aspects of the political economy that the other supply-siders tended to dismiss. Whatever the reason, Stockman was creating some distance between himself and the supply-side purists; eventually, he would become the target of their nasty barbs. For his part, Stockman began to disparage the grand theory as a kind of convenient illusion—new rhetoric to cover old Republican doctrine.

"The hard part of the supply-side tax-cut is dropping the top rate from 70 to 50 percent—the rest of it is a secondary matter," Stockman explained. "The original argument was that the top bracket was too high, and that's having the most devastating effect on the economy. Then, the general argument was that, in order to make this palatable as a political matter, you had to bring down all the brackets. But, I mean, Kemp-Roth was always a Trojan horse to bring down the top rate."

A Trojan horse? This seemed a cynical concession for Stockman to make in private conversation while the Reagan Administration was still selling the supply-side doctrine to Congress. Yet he was conceding what the liberal Keynesian critics had argued from the outset—the supply-side theory was not a new economic theory at all but only new language and argument to conceal a hoary old Republican doctrine: give the tax-cuts to the top brackets, the wealthiest individuals and largest enterprises, and let the good effects "trickle down" through the economy to reach everyone else. Yes, Stockman conceded, when one stripped away the new rhetoric emphasizing across-the-board cuts, the supply-side theory was really new clothes for the unpopular doctrine of the old Republican orthodoxy. "It's kind of hard to sell 'trickle down,' " he explained, "so the supply-side formula was the only way to get a tax policy that was really 'trickle down.' Supply-side is 'trickle-down' theory."

But the young budget director once again misjudged the political context. The scaled-down version of the administration's tax bill would need to carry a few "ornaments" in order to win—a special bail-out to help the troubled savings-and-loan industry, elimination of the so-called marriage penalty—but he was confident that the Reagan majority would hold and he could save $70 billion against those out-year deficits. The business lobbyists would object, he conceded, when they saw the new Republican version of depreciation allowances, but the key congressmen were "on board," and the package would hold.

In early June, it fell apart. The tax lobbyists of Washington, when they saw the outlines of the Reagan tax bill, mobilized the business community, the influential economic sectors from oil to real estate. In a matter of days, they created the political environment in which they flourish best—a bidding war between the two parties. First the Democrats revealed that their tax bill would be more generous than Reagan's in its depreciation rules. Despite Stockman's self-confidence, the White House quickly retreated —scrapped its revised and leaner proposal, and began matching the Democrats, billion for billion, in tax concessions. The final tax legislation would yield, in total, an astounding revenue loss for the federal government of $750 billion over the next five years.

Stockman, with his characteristic ability to adjust his premises to new political realities, at first insisted that the White House cave-in on the business-depreciation issue was of no consequence to his budget problems, since the major impact of the concessions would hit the period 1985 and 1986, beyond the budget years he was struggling with.

Nevertheless, Stockman conceded that the administration had flinched, sending a clear signal to the political interests that it would respond to pressure. "I think we're in trouble on the tax bill," he said in mid-June, "because we started with the position that this was a policy-based bill . . . that we weren't going to get involved in the tax-bill brokering of special-interest claims. But then we made the compromise. . . . My fear now is that, if we do that too many times, it becomes clear to the whole tax-lobby constituency in Washington that we will deal with them one at a time, and then you'll find their champions on the tax-writing committees, especially Finance, swinging into action, and we are going to end up back-pedaling so fast that we will have the 'Christmas tree' bill before we know it."

That was an astute forecast of what unfolded over the next six weeks. Stockman both participated in the process and privately denounced it. But he was not fully engaged in the political scramble for tax concessions, because he was preoccupied with controlling another political auction already under way: the furious bumping-and-trading for the final budget-cutting measure, the reconciliation bill. The thirteen authorizing committees of the House were drawing up the legislative parts to comply with the budget instructions voted by the House in May; simultaneously, the Republican minority members of those committees were drawing up their alternatives, which would become pieces of the administration's alternative—"Son of Gramm-Latta." Stockman was working closely with the Republican drafting in the House, but at the same time he was trying to keep the specific cuts and policy changes in line with the work of the Republican committee chairmen in the Senate. Stockman had a believable nightmare: if House and Senate produced drastically different versions of the final reconciliation measure, there could be a conference committee between the two chambers that would include hundreds of members and months of combat over the differences. Failure to settle quickly could sink the entire budget-cutting enterprise.

Some of the Democratic committee chairmen were playing the "Washington Monument game" (a metaphor for phony budget cuts, in which the National Park Service, ordered to save money, announces that it is closing the Washington Monument). The Education and Labor Committee made deep cuts in programs that it knew were politically sacred: Head Start and impact aid for local schools, and care for the elderly. The Post Office and Civil Service Committee proposed closing 5,000 post offices. Stockman could deal with those ploys—indeed, he felt they strengthened his hand—but he was weakened on other fronts. Again, he had to hold all Republicans and win several dozen of the "boll weevils"—to demonstrate that Ronald Reagan controlled the House. It was not a matter of trading with liberal constituencies and their representatives; Stockman had to do his trading with the conservatives. "In that kind of game," he said, "everybody can ask a big price for one vote."

The final pasted-together measure would be several thousand pages of legislative action and, Stockman feared, another version of the Trojan horse—"a Trojan horse filled full of all kinds of budget-busting measures and secondary agendas."

A group of twenty northern and midwestern, more moderate Republicans, who organized themselves as "gypsy moths" as a counterweight to the "boll weevils," threatened defection. In the end, concessions were made: $350 million more for Medicaid, $400 million more for home-heating subsidies for the poor, $260 million in mass-transit operating funds, more money for Amtrak and Conrail. The administration agreed to put even more money into the nuclear-power project that Stockman loathed, the Clinch

River fast-breeder reactor. It accepted a large authorization for the Export-Import Bank, and more.

Stockman tried to keep everything in line. When he agreed with House Republicans to restore $100 million or so to Amtrak, he had to go back and alert Bob Packwood, of Oregon, chairman of the Senate committee. "The Senate level which his committee tentatively voted out would have shut down a train in Oregon," Stockman said, "and he didn't relish the prospect of not being able to defend his train in the Senate and have it put back in by House Republicans."

In private, the budget director claimed that these new spending figures that Republicans had agreed upon for the various federal programs were not final but merely authorization ceilings, which could be reduced later on, when the appropriations bills for departments and agencies worked their way through the legislative process. "It doesn't mean that you've lost ground," he said blithely of his compromises, "because in the appropriations process we can still insist on $100 million (or whatever other figures appeared in the original Reagan budget) and veto the bill if it goes over. . . . On these authorizations, we can give some ground and then have another run at it."

This codicil of Stockman's was apparently not communicated to the Republicans with whom he was making deals. They presumed that the final figures negotiated with Stockman were final figures. Later on, they discovered that the budget director didn't agree. When in September the President announced a new round of reductions, $13 billion in across-the-board cuts for fiscal year 1982, the ranks of his congressional supporters accused Stockman of breaking his word. In private, some used stronger language. The new budget cuts Stockman prepared in September did, indeed, scrap many of the agreements he negotiated in June when he was collecting enough votes to pass the President's reconciliation bill. In the political morality that prevails in Washington, this was regarded as dishonorable behavior, and Stockman's personal standing was damaged.

"Piranhas," Stockman called the Republican dealers. Yet he was a willing participant in one of the rankest trades—his casual promise that the Reagan Administration would not oppose revival of sugar supports, a scandalous price-support loan program killed by Congress in 1979. Sugar subsidies might not cost the government anything, but could cost consumers $2 to $5 billion. "In economic principle, it's kind of a rotten idea," he conceded. Did Ronald Reagan's White House object? "They don't care, over in the White House. They want to win."

This process of trading, vote by vote, injured Stockman in more profound ways, beyond the care or cautions of his fellow politicians. It was undermining his original moral premise—the idea that honest free-market conservatism could unshackle the government from the costly claims of interest-group politics in a way that was fair to both the weak and the strong. To reject weak claims from powerful clients—that was the intellectual credo that allowed him to hack away so confidently at wasteful social programs, believing that he was being equally tough-minded on the wasteful business subsidies. Now, as the final balance was being struck, he was forced to concede in private that the claim of equity in shrinking the government was significantly compromised if not obliterated.

The final reconciliation measure authorized budget reductions of $35.1 billion, about $6 billion less than the President's original proposal, though Stockman and others said the difference would be made up through shrinking "off-budget" programs, which are not included in the appropriations process. The block grants and reductions and caps that Reagan proposed were partially successful—some sixty major programs were consolidated in different block-grant categories—though Stockman lost several important reforms in the final scrambling, among them the cap on the runaway costs of Medicaid, and user fees for federal waterways. The Reagan Administration eliminated dozens of smaller activities and drastically scaled down dozens of others.

In political terms, it was a great victory. Ronald Reagan became the first President since Lyndon Johnson to demonstrate both the tactical skill and the popular strength to stare down the natural institutional opposition of Congress. Moreover, he forced Congress to slog through a series of unique and painful legislative steps—a genuine reconciliation measure—that undermined the parochial baronies of the committee chairmen. Around Washington, even among the critics who despised what he was attempting, there was general agreement that the Reagan Administration would not have succeeded, perhaps would not even have gotten started, without the extraordinary young man who had a plan. He knew what he wanted to attack and he knew Congress well enough to know how to attack.

Yet, in the glow of victory, why was David Stockman so downcast? Another young man, ambitious for his future, might have seized the moment to claim his full share of praise. Stockman did appear on the Sunday talk shows, and was interviewed by the usual columnists. But in private, he was surprisingly modest about his achievement. Two weeks after selling Congress on the biggest package of budget reductions in the history of the republic, Stockman was willing to dismiss the accomplishment as less significant than the participants realized. Why? Because he knew that much more traumatic budget decisions still confronted them. Because he knew that the budget-resolution numbers were an exaggeration. The total of $35 billion was less than it seemed, because the "cuts" were from an imaginary number—hypothetical projections from the Congressional Budget Office on where spending would go if nothing changed in policy or economic activity. Stockman knew that the CBO base was a bit unreal. Therefore, the total of "cuts" was, too.

Stockman explained: "There was less there than met the eye. Nobody has figured it out yet. Let's say that you and I walked outside and I waved a wand and said, I've just lowered the temperature from 110 to 78. Would you believe me? What this was was a cut from an artificial CBO base. That's why it looked so big. But it wasn't. It was a significant and helpful cut from what you might call the moving track of the budget of the government, but the numbers are just out of this world. The government never would have been up at those levels in the CBO base."

Stockman was proud of what had been changed—shutting down the $4 billion CETA jobs program and others, putting real caps on runaway programs such as the trade adjustment assistance for unemployed industrial workers. "Those were powerful spending programs that have been curtailed," he said, "but there was a kind of consensus emerging for that anyway, even before this administration."

All in all, Stockman gave a modest summary of what had been wrought by the budget victory: "It has really slowed down the momentum, but it hasn't stopped what you would call the excessive growth of the budget. Because the budget isn't something you reconstruct each year. The budget is a sort of rolling history of decisions. All kinds of decisions, made five, ten, fifteen years ago, are coming back to bite us unexpectedly. Therefore, in my judgment, it will take three or four or five years to subdue it. Whether anyone can maintain the political momentum to fight the beast for that long, I don't know."

Stockman, the natural optimist, was not especially optimistic. The future of fiscal conservatism, in a political community where there are "no real conservatives," no longer seemed so promising to him. He spoke in an analytical tone, a sober intellect trying to figure things out, and only marginally bitter, as he assessed what had happened to his hopes since January. In July, he was forced to conclude that, despite the appearance of a great triumph, his original agenda was fading, not flourishing.

"I don't believe too much in the momentum theory any more," he said. "I believe in institutional inertia. Two months of response can't beat fifteen years of political infrastructure. I'm talking about K Street and all of the interest groups in this town, the community of interest groups. We sort of stunned it, but it just went underground for the winter. It will be back. . . . Can we win? A lot of it depends on events and luck. If we got some bad luck, a flareup in the Middle East, a scandal, it could all fall apart."

Stockman's dour outlook was reinforced two weeks later, when the Reagan coalition prevailed again in the House and Congress passed the tax-cut legislation with a final frenzy of trading and bargaining. Again, Stockman was not exhilarated by the victory. On the contrary, it seemed to leave a bad taste in his mouth, as though the democratic process had finally succeeded in shocking him by its intensity and its greed. Once again, Stockman participated in the trading—special tax concessions for oil-lease holders and real-estate tax shelters, and generous loopholes that virtually eliminated the corporate income tax. Stockman sat in the room and saw it happen.

"Do you realize the greed that came to the forefront?" Stockman asked with wonder. "The hogs were really feeding. The greed level, the level of opportunism, just got out of control."

Indeed, when the Republicans and Democrats began their competition for authorship of tax concessions, Stockman saw the "new political climate" dissolve rather rapidly and be replaced by the reflexes of old politics. Every tax lobby in town, from tax credits for wood-burning stoves to new accounting concessions for small business, moved in on the legislation, and pet amendments for obscure tax advantage and profit became the pivotal issues of legislative action, not the grand theories of supply-side tax reduction. "The politics of the bill turned out to be very traditional. The politics put us back in the game, after we started making concessions. The basic strategy was to match or exceed the Democrats, and we did."

But Stockman was buoyant about the political implications of the tax legislation: first, because it put a tightening noose around the size of the government; second, because it gave millions of middle-class voters tangible relief from inflation, even if the stimulative effects on the economy were mild or delayed. Stockman imagined the tax-cutting as perhaps the beginning of a large-scale realignment of political loyalties, away from old-line liberalism and toward Reaganism.

And where did principle hide? Stockman, with his characteristic mixture of tactical cynicism and intellectual honesty, was unwilling to defend the moral premises of what had occurred. The "idea-based" policies that he had espoused at the outset were, in the final event, greatly compromised by the "constituency-based" politics that he abhorred. What had changed, fundamentally, was the list of winning clients, not the nature of the game. Stockman had said the new conservatism would pursue equity, even as it attempted to shrink the government. It would honor just claims and reject spurious ones, instead of simply serving powerful clients over weak clients. He was compelled to agree, at the legislative climax, that the original moral premises had not been served, that the new principles of Reaganism were compromised by the necessity of winning.

"I now understand," he said, "that you probably can't put together a majority coalition unless you are willing to deal with those marginal interests that will give you the votes needed to win. That's where it is fought—on the margins—and unless you deal with those marginal votes, you can't win."

In order to enact Reagan's version of tax reduction, "certain wages" had to be paid, and, as Stockman reasoned, the process of brokering was utterly free of principle or policy objectives. The power flowed to the handful of representatives who could reverse the majority, regardless of the interests they represented. Once the Reagan tacticians began making concessions beyond their policy-based" agenda, it developed that their trades and compromises and giveaways were utterly indistinguishable from the decades of interest-group accommodations that had preceded them, which they so righteously denounced. What was new about the Reagan revolution, in which oil-royalty owners win and welfare mothers lose? Was the new philosophy so different from old Republicanism when the federal subsidies for Boeing and Westinghouse and General Electric were protected, while federal subsidies for unemployed black teenagers were "zeroed out"? One could go on, at great length, searching for balance and equity in the outcome of the Reagan program without satisfying the question; the argument will continue as a central theme of electoral politics for the next few years. For now, Stockman would concede this much: that "weak clients" suffered for their weakness.

"Power is contingent," he said. "The power of these client groups turned out to be stronger than I realized. The client groups know how to make themselves heard. The problem is, unorganized groups can't play in this game."

When Congress recessed for its August vacation and President Reagan took off for his ranch in the West, David Stockman had a surprising answer to one of his original questions: could he prevail in the political arena, against the status quo? His original skepticism about Congress was mistaken; the administration had prevailed brilliantly as politicians. And yet, it also seemed that the status quo, in an intangible sense that most politicians would not even recognize, much less worry over, had prevailed over David Stockman.

V.
"Who Knows?"

Generally, he did not lose his temper, but on a pleasant afternoon in early September, Stockman returned from a meeting at the White House in a terrible black mood. In his ornately appointed office at OMB, he slammed his papers down on the desk and waved away associates. At the Oval Office that afternoon, Stockman had lost the great argument he had been carefully preparing since February: there would be no major retrenchment in the defense budget. Over the summer, Stockman had made converts, one by one, in the Cabinet and among the President's senior advisers. But he could not convince the only hawk who mattered—Ronald Reagan. When the President announced that he would reduce the Pentagon budget by only $13 billion over the next three years, it seemed a pitiful sum compared with what he proposed for domestic programs, hardly a scratch on the military complex, which was growing toward $350 billion a year.

"Defense is setting itself up for a big fall," Stockman had predicted. "If they try to roll me and win, they're going to have a huge problem in Congress. The pain level is going to be too high. If the Pentagon isn't careful, they are going to turn it into a priorities debate in an election year."

Two days later, when we met for another breakfast

conversation, Stockman had recovered from his anger. The argument over the defense budget, he insisted crankily, was a tempest stirred up by the press. The defense budget was never contemplated as a major target for savings. When Stockman was reminded of his earlier claims and predictions—how he would attack the Pentagon's bloated inefficiencies, assisted by a clear-eyed secretary of defense —he shrugged and smiled thinly.

Autumn was cruel to David Stockman's idea of how the world should work. The summer, when furious legislative trading was under way, had tattered his moral vision of government. Politics, in the dirty sense, had prevailed. Now he was confronted with more serious possibilities— the failure of the economic strategy and the political unraveling that he had feared from the beginning. On Capitol Hill, where Stockman was admired and envied for his nimble mind, where even critics conceded that his presence in the Cabinet was essential to Ronald Reagan's opening victories, politicians of both parties were beginning to reach a different conclusion about him. Despite the wizardry, Stockman did not have all the answers, after all. The wizard was prepared to agree.

His failed expectations were derived from many events. In August, when enactment of the Reagan program was supposed to create a boom, instead, the financial markets sagged. Interest rates went still higher, squeezing the various sectors of the American economy. Real-estate sales were dead, and the housing industry was at a historic low point. The same was true for auto sales. Farmers complained about the exorbitant interest demanded for annual crop loans. Hundreds of savings-and-loan associations were at the edge of insolvency. The treasury secretary, perhaps also losing his original faith in the supply-side formulation, suggested that it was time for the Federal Reserve Board to loosen up on its tight monetary policy. Donald Regan saw a recession aproaching.

Stockman's prospects for balancing the budget were getting worse, not better. The optimistic economic forecast made in January to improve his original budget projections came back to haunt him in September. The inflation rate was down considerably (a prediction fortuitously correct because of oil and grain prices) but interest rates were not: the cost of federal borrowing and debt payments went still higher.

Stockman was boxed in, and he knew it. Unable to cut defense or Social Security or to modify the overly generous tax legislation, he was forced to turn back to the simple arithmetic of the federal budget—and cut even more from that smaller slice of the federal dollar that pays for government operations and grants and other entitlements. For six months, Stockman had been explaining to "the West Wing guys" that this math wouldn't add. When Reagan proposed his new round of $16 billion in savings, the political outrage confirmed the diagnosis. Stockman was accused of breaking the agreements he had made in June: Senate Republicans who had accepted the "magic asterisk" so docilely were now talking of rebellion—postponing the enormous tax reductions they had just enacted. While the White House promised a war of vetoes ahead, intended to demonstrate "fiscal control," Stockman knew that even if those short-range battles were won, the budget would not be balanced.

Disappointed by events and confronted with potential failure, the Reagan White House was developing a new political strategy: wage war with Congress over the budget issues and, in 1982, blame the Democrats for whatever goes wrong.

The budget director developed a new wryness as he plunged gamely on with these congressional struggles; it was a quality more appealing than certitude. Appearing before the House Budget Committee, Stockman listed a new budget item on his deficit sheet, drolly labeled "Inaction on Social Security." With remarkable directness and no "magic asterisks," he described the outlook: federal deficits of $60 billion in each of the next three years. Some analysts thought his predictions were modest. In the autumn of 1981, despite his great victories in Congress, Ronald Reagan had not as yet produced a plausible answer to John Anderson's question.

Still, things might work out, Stockman said. They might find an answer. The President's popularity might carry them through. The tax-cuts would make people happy. The economy might start to respond, eventually, to the stimulation of the tax-cuts. "Who knows?" Stockman said. From David Stockman, it was a startling remark. He would continue to invent new scenarios for success, but they would be more complicated and cloudy than his original optimism. "Who knows?" The world was less manageable than he had imagined; this machine had too many crazy moving parts to incorporate in a single lucid theory. The "random elements" of history—politics, the economy, the anarchical budget numbers—were out of control.

Where did things go wrong? Stockman kept asking and answering the right questions. The more he considered it, the more he moved away from the radical vision of reformer, away from the wishful thinking of supply-side economics, and toward the "old-time religion" of conservative economic thinking. Orthodoxy seemed less exciting than radicalism, but perhaps Stockman was only starting into another intellectual transition. He had changed from farm boy to campus activist at Michigan State, from Christian moralist to neo-conservative at Harvard; once again, Stockman was reformulating his ideas on how the world worked. What had he learned?

"The reason we did it wrong—not wrong, but less than the optimum—was that we said, Hey, we have to get a program out fast. And when you decide to put a program of this breadth and depth out fast, you can only do so much. We were working in a twenty or twenty-five-day time frame, and we didn't think it all the way through. We didn't add up all the numbers. We didn't make all the thorough, comprehensive calculations about where we really needed to come out and how much to put on the plate the first time, and so forth. In other words, we ended up with a list that I'd always been carrying of things to be done, rather than starting the other way and asking, What is the overall fiscal policy required to reach the target?''

That regret was beyond remedy now; all Stockman could do was keep trying on different fronts, trying to catch up with the shortcomings of the original Reagan prospectus. But Stockman's new budget-cutting tactics were denounced as panic by his former allies in the supply-side camp. They now realized that Stockman regarded them as "overly optimistic" in predicting a painless boom through across-the-board tax reduction. "Some of the naive supply-siders just missed this whole dimension," he said. "You don't stop inflation without some kind of dislocation. You don't stop the growth of money supply in a three-trillion-dollar economy without some kind of dislocation . . . Supply-side was the wrong atmospherics—not wrong theory or wrong economics, but wrong atmospherics . . . The supply-siders have gone too far. They created this nonpolitical view of the economy, where you are going to have big changes and abrupt turns, and their happy vision of this world of growth and no inflation with no pain.''

The "dislocations" were multiplying across the nation, creating panic among the congressmen and senators who had just enacted this "fiscal revolution." But Stockman now understood that no amount of rhetoric from Washington, not the President's warmth on television nor his own nimble testimony before congressional hearings, would alter the economic forces at work. Tight monetary control should continue, he believed, until the inflationary fevers were sweated out of the economy. People would be hurt. Afterward, after the recession, perhaps the supply-side effects could begin—robust expansion, new investment, new jobs. The question was whether the country or its elected representatives would wait long enough.

His exasperation was evident: "I can't move the system any faster. I can't have an emergency session of Congress to say, Here's a resolution to cut the permanent size of government by 18 percent, vote it up or down. If we did that, it would be all over. But the system works much more slowly. But what can I do about it? Okay? Nothing. So I'm not going to navel-gaze about it too long."

Still trying, still energetic, but no longer abundantly optimistic, Stockman knew that congressional anxieties over the next election were already stronger, making each new proposal more difficult. "The 1982 election cycle will tell us all we need to know about whether the democratic society wants fiscal control in the federal government," Stockman said grimly.

The alternative still energized him. If they failed, if inflation and economic disorder continued, the conservative reformers would be swept aside by popular unrest. The nation would turn back toward "statist" solutions, controls devised and administered from Washington. Stockman shrugged at that possibility.

"Whenever there are great strains or changes in the economic system," he explained, "it tends to generate crackpot theories, which then find their way into the legislative channels."

In subsequent months, it became obvious to even the densest politicians in Washington that Stockman's air of gloom was well-founded. Indeed, in preparing his new estimates of the federal budget, Stockman continued to err on the side of wishful thinking. His projections of future deficits were still much too optimistic. The political community, however, after absorbing the shock of reading about his private doubts, began to scrutinize every assumption about fiscal policy more carefully. The young budget director, it was said, had lost his credibility with congressional committees—and rumors of his demise recurred regularly for many months—but the Reagan Administration faced a much larger problem than David Stockman's reputation. The federal budget was out of control.

In December, Stockman assumed a "low profile," less visible in the news media, while he plunged into the new season of decisions: preparing the administration budget for fiscal 1983, the document which would be the new basis for congressional arguments over spending and taxation. When the 1983 budget was unveiled in February, however, it was almost instantly disowned by those who were supposed to support it—the Republican senators and representatives who had pushed the President's program through the summer before. From Senator Domenici, Republican chairman of the Senate budget committee, to House Speaker O'Neill, leader of the Democratic opposition, the response was the same: nobody believed the President's numbers.

In drafting the new budget, Stockman was predicting declining deficits in the years ahead and for political effect he had labored especially hard to produce a projected deficit for 1983 below the traumatic figure of $100 billion. His final deficit estimate was $92 billion, but critics on Capitol Hill and in the press quickly picked it apart. The deficit assumed all sorts of things which simply were not going to happen, such as a doubling in the revenue from federal oil and gas leases. Moreover, in the design of the budget, Stockman was attempting precisely what he had told the "West Wing guys" last summer would be politically impossible—another round of drastic cuts in the operating arms of government and the grants-in-aid programs. The budget proposed another $60 billion in reductions for domestic social programs in order to reach a deficit below $100 billion, but the immediate political judgment was that those reductions could not be legislated, especially not in an election year.

If the gimmicks were set aside and the Congress did nothing to revise its commitments to tax reduction, the federal budget deficit for 1983 might be twice Stockman's original estimate—and rising, not shrinking, in subsequent years. After several months of back-and-forth, even the President was compelled to concede this. By summer, all the contesting parties had agreed upon a new and more realistic estimate of the federal deficit if nothing was changed: $182 billion in 1983, climbing to $233 billion by 1985.

In short, the Reagan Administration had trapped itself in the same dizzying arithmetic which had confounded fiscal management under its predecessors. Only it was worse. The recession not only postponed beyond anyone's certain prediction the economic growth which might restore lost revenue from the tax-cutting, but it also raised the costs of government on the spending side. The cost of interest payments on new federal borrowing, instead of declining as hoped, stayed high with the high interest rates.

Even liberal Democrats who had never been known to worry excessively over deficit spending began to speak ominously of a "possible catastrophe" for the economy. By the summer months, the congressional leaders of both parties were engaged in a new kind of struggle. The main objective was not in dispute—undoing the disastrous effects of last year's budget-and-tax legislation—but the arguments inspired the most intense kind of political questions: who would pay? Would Congress finally address the question of Social Security reforms, freezing the rise of benefits in order to shrink the deficits? Or would it do what is normally unthinkable in an election year—raise taxes? And whose taxes would be raised, the consumers or corporations, the users of inland waterways or the automobile owners who buy gasoline? The numbers of the rising deficits suggested that Congress had no choice. It had to do all these painful things and many more in order to reverse the trends. Cynics assumed, despite the circumstances and the atmosphere of crisis, that some of the hard choices would be postponed until after the November election. Cynics expected that the Congress would then include many lame-duck Republican members who would be more willing to brave the public wrath.

Congress did the unexpected: with the President's reluctant acceptance, it passed a major tax increase in an election year, recovering about $100 billion of what had been given away in tax cuts the year before. It was not nearly enough. Nor were the three smaller tax increases legislated in subsequent years. In 1985, just as Stockman had feared, the federal government spent $210 billion more than it collected in revenue, an unprecedented deficit. When Reagan took office, the outstanding national debt was about $1 trillion, the accumulated deficits of every President before him. Five years later, the debt was close to $2 trillion.

Conclusion

I.
Failed Magic

Every political decision of consequence is implicitly an act of prophesy, a prediction about the future. And the modern American president, despite the legalisms of his office, will cloak his important policies with an aura of inevitability, just as ancient tribal kings invoked the authority of myth and magic. The wise leader, it is presumed, can see into the future, more clearly than others, and he will lead the people there safely. Indeed, if the people will only believe, the leader can make the future happen.

Murray N. Rothbard, the libertarian economist, among others, has provided a succinct critique of this process of mystification:

"Americans have long shown an inclination to invest the President with mythic powers and significance not even accurately attributable to absolute monarchs and tribal chiefs of yore. Whatever happens in any era, in the economy, the society, or the culture as well as to all individual goals and aspirations is loaded onto this chimerical figure. The President becomes the embodiment of the entire country, even of much of the globe. But in that case, for *us* to be great, we must have a Great President; hence the continuing quest for chief executives who can be made to fit the mold of the mythic hero. We have heard much in recent decades of the dangers of 'elitist history'; but this is elitist history gone berserk.''

The mythic image which Ronald Reagan offered the American public sounds faintly silly when it is described in the abstract, yet it pulled powerfully in concert with all that he was promising Americans. He was the cowboy from the West. He was going to defend the sacred values of the frontier, individualism and opportunity, freedom. Some of his campaign posters actually depicted him as a cowboy. His political managers regularly exploited the image, posing him on horseback or mending fences at his ranch in California. Of course, everyone knew Reagan was not a *real* cowboy; he was a former movie actor turned politician. But strangely enough, that enhanced the symbolic message, for the West which Ronald Reagan promised to restore to American public values was not the real frontier. It was the mythic one from the movies, where the singular hero goes forth to defend good against the forces of evil and triumphs in a dramatic showdown. Against all the contrary evidence, Americans would still like to believe that this is the essential quality of the presidency.

I emphasize the non-rational elements of Ronald Reagan's political leadership because, more than any other particulars, this core of myth and magic comes closest to explaining what happened to the Reagan presidency in its management of the national economy. Given the dense details of David Stockman's ''education,'' the tactical infighting in Congress, and the strategic errors in drafting the budget, one expects to find more tangible reasons. It is easy enough to analyze the many political transactions and discover the pivotal mistakes. Or even to examine Stockman's personality, an intriguing composite of idealism and cynicism, and identify the flaws in his moral vision. This will yield certain insights but miss the larger truth: the political decision-making in Washington in 1981 was guided at a deeper level by mythic qualities and ancient rhythms. In a society that demands rational explanations, that seeks self-justification in logical answers, America's major political institutions were enthralled in a brief convulsion of blind faith.

David Stockman, despite his hyperactive skill with numbers, was a captive of faith. So was the President, so were his other economic advisers. The American public, which always confers renewed faith upon its new leader, wanted also to believe this genial man in the White House had discovered a painless path to that abundant future he promised. Other political leaders, the senators and representatives whose own calculations cast doubt on the President's prophecies, were swept along by the willing suspension of disbelief. The Vice President, in a campaign phrase he lived to regret, had called it "voodoo economics." The Republican majority leader of the Senate called it a "riverboat gamble." Still, knowing this, they believed and took the plunge.

The explanation, I think, lies deeper than the tactical brilliance of the President and his lieutenants, though they were brilliant in their conduct of the legislative struggle. The President offered, first of all, a simple and powerful myth—the vision of laissez-faire—which is still alluring to the American spirit of individualism, despite the many realistic contradictions which history has accumulated. The government would get off everyone's back, it would step back and let everyone prosper, each on his own terms. This message was intimately conveyed into every living room by a skillful performer in the modern medium, a leader who seemed a convincing human being on the TV screen, warm and virtuous. People recognized Ronald Reagan as familiar, the way he talked, the common values he espoused, and they trusted him.

But a modern leader must be more than likeable: he

must invoke the mystery of experts. Reagan's vision of the future was confirmed by computer models, blessed by the technical competence of his young new advisers with young new ideas. Their new idea—the policies known collectively as "supply-side" economics—brashly defied the old rules of fiscal management and promised unconventional results. At its crudest level, this new theory did sound like magic: by reducing everyone's tax rates, the government would actually collect more in taxes. But the "supply-side" argument was forceful because it resonated so neatly with Reagan's larger themes of conservative reform. Finally, the new President skillfully created his own aura of inevitability, mobilizing popular sentiment so effectively that it overpowered the doubters. Even rival skeptics began to think that perhaps Ronald Reagan *did* see the future.

None of this would have been possible, of course, without the necessary preconditions of confusion and disarray in the community of political ideas. Throughout the 1970s, as the economy lurched back and forth from recession to inflation, the orthodox rules of fiscal management failed to produce the sustained economic growth needed for political stability. The liberal responses to economic disorders seemed increasingly hyperactive and extemporaneous. As each new ailment developed in one sector of the economy or another, the Democratic majority would invent a new program to deal with it, usually a subsidy from Washington, either direct or indirect. This approach not only wasn't working, but each new program aroused new resentments from those who did not share in its benefits and a greater appetite among special-interest groups for government-financed remedies for their problems.

Ronald Reagan promised change, or at least the illusion of change. As a candidate, he ran *against* government. Government was not the solution to every problem; government was the problem. During his long campaign for the presidency, Reagan was usually vague about the precise implications of his ideology; he emphasized a general attack on the government's "waste, fraud and mismanagement," but evaded direct statements about which particular interests and which citizens would suffer as he whittled back the size of the central government. Nevertheless, the critique was in harmony with widespread public sentiment, and it also intersected with the elite opinion in Washington. While old-line liberals would resist on every front, a sizeable portion of congressional Democrats, perhaps even a majority of them, felt that Reagan's sense of direction was right, even if they did not share his ultimate goal. The domestic social spending in the federal budget actually peaked in 1978 and began declining as a share of federal spending. As Stockman observed, many of the liberal programs which Reagan attacked were already under assault in the closing years of the Carter Administration.

But, as Stockman also observed, the crucial turning point was the ideological interpretation applied to the 1980 election results. The close analyses of the Reagan landslide made by public-opinion experts generally do not support the conclusion that the American people were voting for a sharp turn toward laissez-faire; the factors which elected Reagan and turned the Senate over to Republican control were more complicated than that. The strongest one was the sense of disappointment with Jimmy Carter. While a large number of liberal senators were defeated by right-wing Republicans, most of those defeated Democrats ran far ahead of Carter in their states and were defeated by narrow margins. The implication was clear: if the presidential contest had been closer, many liberals would have been returned to office.

Nevertheless, the election returns were traumatic for the Democratic Party, particularly the loss of control of the Senate. That not only changed the power equation between the White House and Congress—a new reality which the Republicans understood and exploited before the Democratic leaders could grasp the implications—but the Reagan landslide also challenged the reigning assumptions about the future of political ideas. Caught by surprise, having underestimated this aging actor and his homely conservative bromides, ma.y Democrats were plunged into doubt about their own beliefs. The old orthodoxy, if not wiped out, was abruptly on the defensive and most Democrats calculated that they would wisely not stand directly in the path of this new juggernaut known as the Reagan Revolution. When the President sent his drastic budget cuts to Capitol Hill, the Democratic response was to move dramatically in the same direction. When Reagan proposed his across-the-board tax-cuts, the Democrats tried to negotiate a compromise and, failing that, tried to demonstrate that they, too, were believers in the idea of general tax relief for business and individuals. When orthodoxy is confused, new ideas will fill the vacuum, even new ideas which seem too simple-minded to be effective in this complex society.

While Reagan's uses of myth and magic were uniquely successful, it is important to remember that a milder precedent occurred in 1976 when Jimmy Carter was elected. He offered a different image—a farmer from a small town— but he invoked similar themes of restoration. Carter promised to restore the small-town virtues of decency and honor, openness, fair dealing, simplicity. When one examined the content of his campaign positions, the same vagueness and contradiction were revealed. Yet Americans wanted to believe and they did, for a time. In the end, of course, Carter left the White House a failure. He became President by preaching simple reassurances; at the conclusion he was pleading with the American public to accept the unsatisfying complexities of modern life. By 1980, Carter campaigned on complicated realities; Reagan promised simple solutions.

Inevitably, however, a President *is* like an ancient king.

If his magic fails and the prophecies do not come true, he will lose authority. His words and gestures, his new promises, will begin to sound empty and contrived and, without the myth and magic, he can no longer manipulate the political community to realize his goals. In approximate terms, this happened to Ronald Reagan more swiftly and dramatically than it had to any of his immediate predecessors. By mid-1982, his popularity was sinking rapidly. Then, almost as swiftly, his political fortunes reversed, as economic recovery took hold in 1983. Reagan's magic seemed to be working, after all, and indeed he spoke of the revived economy as a "miracle." The news media took up the theme and amplified it. Reelected in a landslide, the President seemed more popular than any of his modern predecessors. Yet, in practical terms, the kingly authority was not restored. Congress, increasingly, chose its own course in confronting the fiscal disorder. The public asserted its own disfavor for Reagan's annual budgets, and little that he proposed for further shrinkage of federal programs was actually adopted. It all changed with dizzying speed.

This accelerated pace alters the political process in fundamental ways which neither the politicians nor the public has fully absorbed. Both seem disoriented, like actors and audience in a movie that is running jerkily at high speed. The characters and plot seem to lurch forward precariously, everything moving too fast. This is different, fundamentally, from the American past and the political expectations we inherited. In the past, a radical new departure in government policy would undergo years, even decades, of scrutiny and argument, before it surfaced as a popular cause and worked its way into the center ring of policymakers where final decisions reside. A wrong idea, likewise, might live on as established wisdom for many years beyond its effectiveness, sustained by popular ignorance or immutable faith. The political community debated Keynesian economics for thirty years before it was accepted by all sides as the orthodoxy of fiscal management; the new formulations of "supply-side" economics progressed in barely a half dozen years from a small and eclectic circle of advocates to presidential policy.

President Reagan discovered, however, more swiftly than even Jimmy Carter had, that the power of the presidency, secured by promising mythical restoration and fundamental change, immediately collides with enduring forces. There is a special danger, it seems, in a President elected on simplistic homilies: he may come to believe that the people have empowered him to take drastic actions in the name of those values. If so, he soon finds the people abandoning him when the debate gets down to the hard specifics. Thus, Reagan's hard-line Cold War rhetoric, which seemed so popular during the campaign, did not prepare him for the abrupt shift in popular opinion which occurred when his administration deepened U. S. involvement in El Salvador. The voters liked the idea of restoring American prestige and power in the world, but not if it meant actual engagement in another foreign war. Likewise, Reagan's hostility toward the Soviet Union was tempered by events. He disappointed his own right-wing constituencies by declining to take a harder line against the suppression of freedom in Poland (his advisers counseled him that while the suspension of trading and finance with the Soviet bloc nations might satisfy Cold War impulses, it might also set off an international economic crisis). After launching the biggest peacetime buildup of military hardware in history, the Reagan Administration was blindsided by another wave of popular reaction—fear of nuclear war— and was compelled to begin negotiations with the Soviets on arms reductions.

At the same time, of course, the voters who had presumably made an ideological choice in 1980—voting for Reagan's vision of a smaller government in Washington—

were expressing on every front their strong distaste for the actual consequences of his economic policies. By the summer of 1982, the widely-held belief, reflected in public-opinion surveys, was that Reagan was unfair. Instead of helping all Americans, his policies favored the well-to-do. Instead of producing the robust growth he promised, the nation was in recession. The Gallup Poll reported, fifteen months after the Reagan Inauguration, that more Americans disapproved of the President than approved. Yet fifteen months later, his popularity was wholly restored when the economy began to expand and unemployment declined.

The chemistry of the presidency has changed; the center of national politics now seems extraordinarily fluid and vulnerable. Yet each president stumbles into the same trap. In order to get elected in the age of television, the successful video candidate will manipulate words and images to convey a value system of mythological proportions. When he turns to fulfill those promised values with actual policies, however, the TV audience is still watching. The reassuring qualities of his campaign image suddenly become frightening to the viewers. The myth and magic was comforting, even alluring, but the reality is harsh and disappointing. The cowboy who was so likeable as a candidate suddenly seems reckless as a President.

One can blame the politicians for this phenomenon, of course, but the public likes the myths, too. A political candidate, regardless of party or ideology, is likely to take the approach that succeeds, the one that wins elections, and so modern candidates turn to the technology of myth-making—campaign consultants who are TV directors in disguise and the political technocrats who will make their particular magic sound persuasive. That isn't likely to change as long as it wins. The only available remedy, it seems, is for ordinary citizens to understand the elements of magic and why they fail.

II.
The Washington Apprentice

Somewhere in America, undoubtedly, there are intelligent, ambitious farm boys who have read the story of David Stockman and decided that they, too, will be director of the U.S. budget in ten or fifteen years. Or perhaps they will settle for Secretary of Transportation or U.S. senator or whatever. This is not an outrageous goal, if they are bright and aggressive and lucky. One striking quality of Stockman's career is the ease and swiftness with which he moved from an obscure and unpretentious background to the highest circle of power in the federal government. And he did so essentially by ignoring the sort of patient career paths that political tradition would prescribe for one with his ambitions. This pattern is not at all unusual in modern Washington; the channels of power are much more accessible to new participants than one might think. While Stockman's ascendancy was especially deft and dramatic, the departments of government and the congressional staffs on Capitol Hill are networks of similar striving individuals—"staffers" who will become experts in their fields, then use their expertise to win political appointments to important positions. They are the technocrats of public policy, but they espouse partisan loyalties in concert with elected officials; they share influence over policy decisions with their better-known bosses, while nourishing their own plausible ambitions for higher status.

If one looks around the government under Reagan or his immediate predecessors, there are many other examples of "staffers" who climbed to the top or reasonably close. John Lehman, Jr., Secretary of the Navy, began a dozen years ago as a policy analyst at the National Security Council under President Nixon. He moved eventually to the Arms Control and Disarmament Agency under President Ford and, when the Republicans regained the White House, he lobbied successfully for his sub-Cabinet title. Richard Perle, who holds the pivotal post of Assistant Secretary of Defense for International Security Policy, dealt with the same issues for many years as a staff assistant to Senator Henry Jackson. Richard G. Darman apprenticed on several Cabinet staffs under Elliot Richardson before becoming Deputy Assistant to the President, an obscure but influential job in which he monitors every document and memorandum that is set before the President to read. During the Carter Administration, a similar list of technocrats with Democratic loyalties moved in to fill many of the key policy positions. At the Capitol, there is a growing number of new representatives and even a few new senators who prepared for elective office like Stockman, not by working their way up the ladder of local and state political offices, but by first learning the ways of Washington, then going back home to run for office.

In the Carter years, the permanent technocrats came from the other side of the street, ideologically. They were drawn from congressional staffs and also from the networks of "public-interest" activists associated with Ralph Nader and the environmental movement. The staff of Carter's domestic policy council in the White House, though headed by a fellow Georgian, Stuart Eizenstat, was actually a collection of young reformers from Capitol Hill and consumer-environmental groups. William Spring, in charge of labor and manpower training policies, had worked for many years on the same subject, as a committee aide to Senator Gaylord Nelson. Simon Lazarus, formerly at the Federal Communications Commission under reformer Nicholas Johnson, was directing civil service and regulatory reform. Eizenstat himself had been tutored on policymaking in the Johnson Administration. At the State Department and Pentagon, the second rung of Carter appointees followed a similar pattern—young Washington experts on the way up.

To a new administration taking power, these resident experts are valuable for their knowledge of the past. They know, just as Stockman knew, the complex technical background for each major issue, the legislative history, and the conventional arguments on all sides. At the White House, their expertise is especially needed because a newly-elected President is likely to construct an inner circle of advisers who are outsiders to government—political managers and long-faithful campaign aides who know a great deal about the new President and his desires but not so much about running things in Washington. In administration after administration, obscure Americans who are essentially political technicians have been anointed with awesome power: Haldeman and Ehrlichman under Nixon, Jordan and Powell under Carter, Meese and Baker under Reagan. In that setting, the young David Stockmans seem like "old hands." Having studied the practical processes of the permanent government and mastered the operating techniques, they are indispensable to the newcomers.

To succeed in that striving network, one needs special qualities, beyond the obvious ones of intelligence and ambition, which Stockman possessed in fuller measure than most. A policy planner of any sort must be able to dwell comfortably in a world of abstractions—dense argument and analysis, statistical generalizations describing tangible realities in the society—abstractions which would benumb the minds of most Americans. In order to advance in political status, however, the ambitious "staffer" also needs some combination of the contradictory qualities in Stockman's character. Both friends and adversaries would wonder about him: was he an idealist or a cynic? Did he really believe in what he was doing or did he simply love the power? An idealogue or merely an opportunist? The answer always seemed obvious to me: he was both. Stockman brought to the table a coherent set of ideas in which he believed, an ideology reasonably grounded in moral argument. He also brought a politician's cynical understanding of human nature, a pragmatic appreciation for games and how to play them. On balance, Stockman seemed more idealistic, more ideological, than the usual ambitious technocrats, many of whom are much more willing to sacrifice their own set of political ideas in order to attain an influential role. But Stockman was still an opportunistic operator, willing to take risks others would shrink from, to manipulate and trade, to gamble. When Stockman was asked about his rapid rise to power, he explained it as a combination of inspired risk-taking and good luck.

All of these qualities are relevant to understanding what happened in the process which shaped the Reagan economic policy, not so much because Stockman himself was a central figure, but because the presumptions of technocratic politicians, of bold and tough-minded risktaking, created the atmosphere in which the new President's plans were designed and advanced. That environment, we now understand, was fragile and hectic, the opposite of deliberative. And yet the participants cloaked themselves in hyperrational jargon and an intimidating self-confidence which, we now know, concealed a large measure of old-fashioned wishful thinking. This pose of rational certitude was not, of course, invented by David Stockman or the Reagan Administration; it strikes me as a permanent fallacy of technocratic government, a mask recreated by each new generation of policymakers to conceal their own human limitations. The press, incidentally, plays a critical role in keeping the technocratic fallacy alive, by portraying each new wave of policymakers, regardless of party, as bold and tough-minded rationalists. This model goes back at least as far as the Kennedy Administration. When policies fail, the press usually assigns the blame in personal terms, discovering previously unseen flaws in the policymaker's character, but the idea of magic experts survives.

David Stockman's opportunism and his wishful thinking, his ability to manipulate policy abstractions and to play the game of politics, were all marvelously summarized in an advisory memorandum which he wrote in collaboration with Representative Jack Kemp in the weeks following the election victory of 1980. It was an artful document entitled, "Avoiding a GOP Economic Dunkirk" (reprinted as an appendix to this book), which they presented to the President-elect and his closest advisers ostensibly to lay out the dimensions for Reagan economic policy, but mainly as a lobbying tool to persuade the Reagan team that Stockman, the young congressman from Michigan, had all the necessary qualities—boldness, brains, technical brilliance, ideological purity—to become director of OMB. Stockman was the candidate sponsored by Kemp and the "supply-siders," but he had cultivated other support, too. The Heritage Foundation, a New Right think tank which was drafting its own blueprint for dismantling regulatory enforcement, and the Moral Majority, which had its own social agenda, also liked Stockman (endorsements which were surely not won without some commitments from the candidate to do the budget-cutting those groups wanted). In case the "Dunkirk" memorandum did not totally persuade the private circle around Reagan, Stockman and Kemp made certain it received wide distribution and frequent mention in the press. At one point, three newspapers—

the *Washington Post*, the *New York Times*, and the *Washington Star*—each published excerpts of this "confidential" document.

With a brisk sense of urgency and impressive detail, Stockman paid homage to each component of the Republican agenda and its particular objectives: the need for major tax reductions, for across-the-board repeal of regulatory controls on business and industry, for tight monetary control, for dramatic budget-cutting. But the analysis of the economic prospects which Reagan would inherit was wrong on several major points: Stockman predicted another round of crippling price inflation in oil and grain, so-called "commodity shocks" which would blindside every reform the new President envisioned. Instead, both basic commodities were in surplus throughout 1981, and their sagging prices contributed directly to the declining rate of inflation which Reagan achieved. After the Inauguration, cooler heads prevailed, and the President did not adopt the principal recommendation from the "Dunkirk" memo—the suggestion that he should declare a "national economic emergency" to convince the public of the urgency of his cause.

In hindsight, the "Dunkirk" memorandum is still interesting because, despite the errors and exaggerations, it did accurately forecast what would ultimately happen to the Reagan economic recovery program—the continuation of high interest rates which discouraged any new investment and eventually produced recession. Here is an excerpt:

"The preeminent danger is that an initial economic policy package that includes the tax cuts but does not contain *decisive, credible elements* [Stockman's emphasis] on matters of outlay control, future budget authority reduction and a believable plan for curtailing the federal government's massive direct and indirect credit absorption will generate pervasive expectations of a continuing *'Reagan inflation.'* Such a development would almost insure that high interest rates would hang over the economy well into the first year, deadening housing and durable markets and thwarting the industrial capital spending boom required to propel sustained economic growth. Thus, Thatcherization [note: the same economic decline which confronted Margaret Thatcher's Tory government in Britain, employing similar policies] can only be avoided if the initial economic policy package simultaneously spurs the output side of the economy and also elicits a swift downward revision of inflationary expectations in the financial markets.''

The Stockman memo proposed an arresting solution for this dilemma: the magic of decisive political action. If the President acted boldly, it would alter the psychological climate surrounding these economic problems. The skeptics in Wall Street would recognize that a new era of responsible political management had begun in Washington and, hence, alter their own assumptions about future inflation. ''Achieving fiscal control over outlays and Treasury borrowing *cannot be conducted as an accounting exercise* or *exclusively through legislated spending cuts in the orthodox sense*. Only a comprehensive economic package that spurs output and employment growth and lowers inflation expectations and interest rates has any hope of stopping the present hemorrhage.''

Despite the formalistic language of fiscal policy, this was essentially a call to faith. It is a political vision of how symbolic political action might change hearts and minds, rather than an economic argument about how markets work. In hindsight, it seems bizarre that a new administration of supposedly tough-minded Republicans, believing in the hard numbers of free-market transactions, could so easily delude themselves. But this notion was so frequently articulated by so many leading officials of the Reagan Administration in its opening year that it became known popularly as the "theory of expectations." Stockman warned: "Only one remedy is available: an initial administration economic program that is so bold, sweeping, and sustained that it totally dominates the Washington agenda during 1981, holds promise of propelling the economy into vigorous expansion and the financial markets into a bullish psychology, preempts the kind of debilitating distractions outlined above."

The President himself expressed this wishfulness on many occasions as he was urging Congress to enact his tax and budget legislation. Indeed, as final passage of the tax bill was occurring, Reagan told his national audience of TV viewers of bountiful plans for new industrial expansion which he said were already underway. "All of this," he boasted, "was based on anticipation of our program being adopted and put into action."

Those "plans," of course, did not materialize. The following month the long-term bond market stalled out again and a long recession began. Eight months later, the Commerce Department reported soberly that new investments planned by U.S. business for 1982 would actually decline from the previous year; corporate spending for new plant capacity and equipment would be down by .5 percent. Alan Greenspan, the conservative economist who was never an enthusiast of the "theory of expectations," predicted that the commerce forecast would prove to be too optimistic, that capital investment in 1982 would decline by as much as 2.5 percent. Stockman, of course, had already given up on "expectations" as the way to alter financial markets and interest rates. "I changed my mind on that," he said at a luncheon in September 1981. "I do not believe the financial markets buy announcements. They only measure results."

Any financial analyst, advising his clients on long-term investments like corporate bonds, was compelled to look at the numbers for himself. Whatever the President declared on television, whatever glory and hoopla surrounded the congressional victories, the budget numbers still told the same message: the Reagan program had not improved the problem of deficit spending by the federal government, the factor which Stockman feared would produce the continuing ruination of high interest rates. The Reagan policy made that problem much worse. For a bond trader, this sort of tangible reality will not yield to faith.

And yet official Washington, at the highest levels, had persuaded itself. I think there is an important paradox of power involved in this collective self-delusion, the kind of confusion which has recurred in recent administrations and to which the permanent technocrats may be particularly vulnerable. They do live, simultaneously, in a world of abstraction, the realm of ideas which become policies, and also in the arena of political action, where the exertions of politicians provide the connection with tangible results. And it is easy to confuse the two, so that one believes that the exercise of power is itself a symbolic abstraction. This confusion actually magnifies the influence of political action beyond its true dimensions. Political decisions are translated into a symbolic realm where their effects are questionable at best, particularly in influencing economic matters. The national government does, of course, exercise direct and awesome power over the life and commerce of America, but that exercise of power is primarily concrete and direct, not abstract and symbolic.

A political technocrat, whose experience of risk-taking and success has been narrowly confined to the abstract battles of Washington combat, may perceive the messages of politics and government as more potent than they really are. The President makes a television address and the Congress is deluged with mail. The administration proposes new legislation and great special interests tremble. War is averted and the stock market rallies. The cause-and-effect implied by these transactions, at least for the participants, puts Washington at the center of every drama. And every Washington drama puts the participants at the center of power.

As a mode of thinking, the "theory of expectations" has many precedents in previous administrations. The President, as symbolist, will exhort the nation to behave, as in "jawboning" on wage and price restraint. Or the President will take certain bold actions intended to promise or threaten other bold actions to follow. In that manner, the "theory of expectations" resembled the strategy of "graduated escalation" which previous Presidents employed during the war in Indochina—using bombing strikes to deliver diplomatic ultimatums. It was not the bombing itself that would end the war, but the symbolic message that this dramatic action would send to the enemy. Likewise, Reagan's budget cuts by themselves would not reduce federal deficits, but would send the appropriate message to Wall Street, thus producing the economic boom. This particular brand of magic is nearly always less effective than Washington likes to believe. The Viet Cong did not get the message and neither did Wall Street.

III.

The Bewildered Orthodoxy

What exactly did happen? What did the new President do to federal fiscal policy which produced such a storm of confusion, even panic, among the politicians and economists and business leaders? It is important to go back to that simple question, because the President and others continued to obscure the reality with their rhetoric. If one believed Ronald Reagan's explanations, he was merely confronting the inherited chaos which flowed from many years of mismanagement by Democratic-controlled government and, though he never mentioned it, by prior Republican Presidents. Gallantly, he tried to roll back the tide.

"In our budget proposal," he told the nation in another televised address on April 29, 1982, "we had continued the process we started last year of trying to get control of runaway government spending. Deficits over the past few decades have been literally built into the federal structure. The rate of increase in spending was 17 percent when we took office. There's no way that government can pay for increases at that rate without gigantic tax increases each year or borrowing and adding to the national debt. This latter course has been followed for so many years that we now have a trillion-dollar debt."

Later, after blaming the Democrats for recalcitrance,

Reagan got to the bad news—an astonishing admission. His own fiscal stewardship was going to produce federal deficits that would make Jimmy Carter and Gerald Ford, Richard Nixon and Lyndon Johnson, even Harry Truman and Franklin Roosevelt, seem like prudent managers. Of course, Reagan did not put it quite that way. "While I don't believe in the accuracy of long-range projections," he said, "we're required to acknowledge them in our budgeting. They [the projected deficits] stand at $182 billion for 1983, $216 billion in '84 and $233 billion in 1985 if we do nothing about reducing spending." Notwithstanding these staggering numbers, Reagan concluded his speech by earnestly announcing once more that he favored a constitutional amendment to require balanced budgets.

As the President himself conceded, the worst thing about those deficit projections was that they grew larger each year, not smaller. This is the crux of what the Reagan fiscal policy produced. In the preceding decade, as inflation and recession alternately produced their different disorders, each President, from Nixon to Carter, struggled for balance and ended up lurching from one aggravation to another. Still, in their fiscal planning, those Presidents were regularly reassured by the long-term projections. The budget would not be in balance this year but, if one looked to the "out years," it was clear that the lines on the chart representing spending and revenue were converging. The deficits would grow smaller and, in two or three years, if no external forces intervened, the federal budget would be in approximate balance.

Ronald Reagan reversed those lines on the chart. Given the Reagan Administration's combination of tax reductions and budget increases, mainly for defense, no neutral observer could continue to look at the trendlines of future revenue and spending and find any reassurance. The revenue line, instead of moving upward to intersect eventually with the spending line, would be moving away from it during the next five years. That stark reality, once it penetrated the shared wisdom of the business and political elite, is what launched the budget crisis of the Reagan presidency. That is what propelled Republicans and Democrats alike into their frenzied efforts to undo in the summer of 1982 what the Congress had triumphantly enacted in the summer of 1981.

The intriguing question, in hindsight, is how this could have happened. How could so many grown men and women share in the collective delusion? The budget figures, after all, were not secret and, despite the celebrated juggling of numbers by Stockman and others, as well as the reassuring promises from the President, the new trendlines were obvious to any disinterested analyst who sat down and studied what Congress and the President had wrought in terms of tax-and-budget changes. This is what Wall Street understood.

Part of the answer, I think, lies in the magic of a new theory, the doctrine of "supply-side" economics, which promised a fundamental redirection of the national economy, without pain or dislocation. As Stockman discovered, somewhat before others around him, this was naïve. Still, to understand how the political community could embrace the wish so blindly, one must understand the policies the "supply-siders" proposed and what they thought would happen.

After the stagnant seventies, the status quo seemed bankrupt. The operating principles of Keynesian demand-side economic management failed to provide the crucial constant of American politics: economic growth. Instead, the rise of American productivity slowed and finally seemed to stop. Succeeding governments fumbled between curing inflation and curing unemployment, but the orthodox measures seemed not to work any longer. If monetary growth was held tight and federal spending dampened, that cured inflation temporarily but produced intolerable unemployment. If the government pumped up the economy with additional spending and loosened up on the money supply, that reduced unemployment but launched another season of double-digit inflation. Both indexes—inflation and unemployment—ricochet upward through the decade so that each time the aggravation occurred it was worse than before.

When orthodoxy fails, the political effects are destabilizing. Washington was weary and frustrated by the erratic policymaking, epitomized most dramatically by Jimmy Carter's last year in office when he seemed to change direction every other month (and managed to combine both a recession and double-digit inflation). Carter's Council of Economic Advisers, dominated by middle-of-the-road Keynesians, had been wrong every quarter for four years in its prognosis and predictions. If the old expertise was wrong, then perhaps it was time for new experts.

In that setting, the unconventional arguments surrounding "supply-side" economics were appealing even to those who never fully subscribed to the theoretical foundations. In the political realm, the atmospherics created by a new idea may be as influential as the substantive theory; one carries the other forward. It is never clear how deeply the political actors understand the underlying argumentation. The "supply-side" school, in any case, proposed to throw out the old operating rules; practical experience had told the politicians that the old rules weren't working.

The invention of the "supply-side" theory is itself a case study of intellectual guerrillas who successfully assaulted the traditional bastions of policy formulation and managed in a few years to popularize their thinking. By all accounts, the movement began in the early 1970s with a journalist, Jude Wanniski, who was not trained as an economist but became absorbed, even obsessed, by the possibilities of applying hybrid solutions to contemporary economic disorders. Wanniski began with casual seminars with a young California economist named Arthur Laffer, and later with the classical economist Robert Mundell of Columbia University. As conversations evolved into policy formulations, Wanniski became a one-man organizer for a growing network of like-minded economists and politicians. As an editorial writer for the *Wall Street Journal*, he persuaded his boss, Robert Bartley, editor of the *Journal's* editorial page, to give the new ideas an airing and, in time, Bartley became an apostle himself. The *Wall Street Journal*, long identified as the voice of conservative orthodoxy, became the principal pulpit for radical new thinking. Bartley's editorials and the opinion pieces he published laid out the case for the new direction and cheered on politicians like Jack Kemp and Stockman who were espousing the "supply-side" doctrine. Bartley, another student of economics without formal academic credentials, liked to tell interviewers how he viewed his zealous mentor, Wanniski: "In college, I had a bacteriology teacher who gave me a great insight into life. He said that if you were transported back into time and met Pasteur and Koch, you'd probably think they were just like a lot of other nuts—except they were right."

In its broadest form, the "supply-side" idea was not "nuts." It argued that the fallacy of Keynesian fiscal management was to focus exclusively on the "demand side" of the national economy, consumer spending, and that it was preoccupied only with making sure, to put it crudely, that people had enough money to spend so they would buy the goods and services that kept commerce and industry healthy and growing. Wanniski and the others argued that the federal government's economic managers must shift their attention and influence to the "supply side," the productive capacity in the economy that supplied the goods and services. Federal policy under the Keynesian orthodoxy, particularly the marginal tax rates on income from both wages and investments, was the principal cause of disorder, they believed. The federal income tax would take half of each extra dollar earned from work at the top bracket and 70 percent of each extra dollar earned from capital investment such as stocks and bonds. This deadened economic growth by dampening everyone's incentive for additional income from both work and investment. The federal government, meanwhile, made matters worse through its monetary policy, "monetizing" the national deficits by simply printing more money at the Federal Reserve Board and thus adding inflation to the stagnation. That is a generalized outline, to be sure, but in that broad formulation the "supply-side" argument was triumphant and, indeed, despite the debacle of Reagan's economic policy, the "supply-side" critique continued triumphant as a general sentiment. With only minor dissent from the left, the political community remained convinced of the soundness of the "supply-side" emphasis: attend to capital investment as the way to revive the growth of productivity in the U.S. economy and, simultaneously, maintain tight monetary control over the growth in the money supply as the weapon against inflation.

In the more specific terms of policy, however, the "supply-side" argument advanced a logical contradiction which, ultimately, produced the crisis. It hybridized two opposite approaches to government economic management into one policy and guaranteed a collision. While the Federal Reserve Board, under Chairman Paul Volcker, exercised its tight monetary control (a direction actually initiated in late 1979), the President and Congress would initiate a loose fiscal policy, putting billions of dollars into the hands of consumers as well as investors to spend. Thus, according to the old orthodoxy, the government was trying to go in opposite directions at the same time: a monetary policy that would hold back the economy and squeeze out the inflation and a federal budget that would pump up the economy for robust growth. Could the two be

effectively combined? The core of the "supply-side" thinking answered yes: while monetary control melted away the
inflationary disorders, the across-the-board tax reductions
on the fiscal side would provide incentives for real investment in real growth. Thus liberated, citizens would work
harder and stop putting their money in hedges against
inflation—money-market funds or antiques or precious
metals—and start investing it in a productive capacity.
This hybrid formulation, as Bartley explained to me, was
the single premise which made the "supply-side" thinking
different from its intellectual predecessors, both liberal and
conservative. In a way, "supply-siders" proposed to marry
the two and enjoy the best of both worlds. Or at least to
see what would happen.

It is not evident, to put it mildly, that many of the
political actors of Washington fully appreciated the logical
contradiction inherent in the "supply-side" case when
they embarked on their season of tax-cutting. Certainly,
many mainstream economists did, as well as the best
professional critics in the press. But this was a theoretical
argument among theoreticians and their warnings sounded
like the tired quibbling of rejected experts. Besides, the
"supply-siders" had attractive interior arguments which
added luster to their case and distracted politicians from
the theoretical abstractions. One of these was known as the
Laffer Curve.

Wanniski likes to tell a possibly apochryphal anecdote
about how the Laffer Curve was first drawn on a cocktail
napkin while he and Arthur Laffer explored the origins of
their theory. Laffer's insight was, like other aspects of
"supply-side," a reasonable proposition in its most general form: at some unknown point, as the government
continued to raise its rates of taxation, it would actually
begin to receive less revenue. At the extremes, this curve
of tax rates and revenue seemed logically indisputable.
After all, if the government set the income tax rate at 100

percent of income, it would most likely collect nothing in taxes. Likewise, if the tax rates reached the theoretical point where they seemed confiscatory to the taxpayers, surely that would discourage them from seeking additional income since it would only be lost to the government. If the marginal tax rates in the United States had already reached that point, the top of the Laffer Curve where raising the rates further would only shrink the amount of revenue collected, then perhaps the reverse effects would flow from lowering the tax rates. Cutting taxes would increase the incentive to work and to earn additional income from investments; the increased economic activity would lead to a greater pool of earnings to be taxed and, thus, would yield larger revenues despite the lowered rate. In the argument, this increase became known as the "reflow"—the increased revenue that would come surging back from tax reduction, a phenomenon with a supposed precedent in the tax reductions enacted in the early 1960s by the Kennedy Administration.

There were, however, both theoretical and political weaknesses in the claim. While everyone might agree, at least theoretically, that Laffer was right about the eventual effects of rising tax rates, no one could establish convincingly that the U.S. government had already reached the critical point at the top of the Laffer Curve or beyond. If it hadn't, then reducing tax rates would simply reduce revenues. More to the point, no one could say with any certainty how soon this "reflow" might occur or what revenue it would yield. Would it take six months or a year or several years to recapture the lost revenue? The answer was crucial to the political outcome because, in the meantime, the government would run up horrendous deficits and nervous politicians might lose patience with the experiment (that, incidentally, is why the "theory of expectations" was so useful in the political debate; it conveniently promised an instant response from the tax-paying economy).

I think it is reasonable to surmise that many congressional politicians, even the senators and representatives who enacted Reagan's massive tax-cuts, were never totally convinced by the Laffer Curve. Still, the idea served as a comforting talisman for them and contributed to the self-delusion. Whenever anyone cited the potential consequences of drastically reducing federal tax rates, the specter of huge deficits, the marvelous effects of "reflow" would be cited in rebuttal. No one could prove that this argument was wrong, at least until it had been tried, and it offered such a wonderful cure for the nation's economic ailments. Cut everyone's taxes and nobody gets hurt, not even the government. The purists like Kemp even asserted that reducing the federal spending was an unnecessary pain since the increased revenues would soon wipe out the temporary deficits. The "supply-siders" did concede that some budget reduction was probably required as a practical political matter, in order to reassure those skeptical conservatives who did not truly believe in the new wisdom. (Conservatives were always divided among themselves over the meaning of the Reagan policy. When Stockman conceded that the underlying purpose of "supply side" was identical to the old "trickle down" policy, the "supply-siders" angrily denied this and denounced Stockman, but other more orthodox conservative commentators observed that, of course, Stockman was correct, and why make such a big fuss over it?)

Despite the warnings and misgivings from mainstream economists, Congress went ahead and enacted the general outlines. Conventional opinion, I think, probably assumed that the process of steering the package through Congress would inevitably moderate it, reducing the fiscal impact. Instead, the opposite happened. As Stockman described, the congressional battle turned into a bidding war between the two parties and a gravy train of tax concessions for special interests. The eventual fiscal impact was worse than the original plan envisioned.

What exactly did happen to the economy? Professional students of economics will argue that question for many years to come, but the rough outline seems to be this: while the Federal Reserve's monetary control was already cooling the economy, pushing down inflation and increasing unemployment, the Reagan tax legislation came along and inadvertently exacerbated the situation. The "reflow" did not occur and, instead, the huge deficits dampened the long-range prospects for the new investments that the tax reductions were supposed to encourage. The high interest rates which depress all economic activity, especially long-term bonds, not only stayed high but remained so through the recession, when normally interest rates are expected to fall rapidly. High unemployment and high interest rates— one might say the U.S. economy experienced the worst of both worlds. The two contradictory halves of "supply-side" policy were in collision.

By the spring of 1982, this was more widely understood. Lindley H. Clark, Jr., economics columnist with the *Wall Street Journal*, wrote a front-page "Outlook" piece which began: "A common complaint about current economic policy is that money is too tight and the budget is too loose: monetary and fiscal policy are mismatched." The Brookings Institution in Washington, which some regarded as a redoubt for the discredited Keynesians, issued its annual analysis of federal budget policy, "Setting National Priorities: The 1983 Budget," which warned:

"Fiscal and monetary policies appear to be on a collision course in the years immediately ahead. . . . In circumstances such as those now prevailing in the economy, output and employment may grow for brief periods. But any sustained expansion is likely to be choked off by rising interest rates, as increasing credit demands run up against the tight monetary targets. This is what happened in the aftermath of the 1980 recession and the experience is likely to be repeated in the coming years unless the mix of fiscal and monetary policies is significantly altered."

Volcker, the Federal Reserve chairman, promised no retreat on his end, but he told a luncheon audience of New York business executives of his concerns about the other end, the way Congress and the President had managed the federal budget. "You get larger deficits each year, rather than smaller ones," Volcker complained. "This is a unique situation in terms of the American economy, and this is what is dangerous about current fiscal policy. I know of no action that would be more important and more effective in dealing with short- and long-term economic problems and with high interest rates than bringing the deficits under control."

President Reagan was acclaimed, nonetheless, because his administration made spectacular progress against inflation—from double-digit price escalation in 1981 to less than 4 percent two years later. This was no "miracle," however, and required no new theory of economics. Prices fell sharply because the Federal Reserve restrained the money supply, driving up interest rates and pushing the economy into a severe recession. Unemployment reached close to 11 percent and bankruptcies multiplied by the tens of thousands. It is an old-fashioned cure for inflation and it is never painless.

Economists and congressional politicians, in any case, became frightened by a larger possibility: the Reagan fiscal policy might lead to economic disorders far worse than a recession or high inflation. This fear was muted in the public dialogue, lest the discussion of it become a self-fulfilling prophecy, but there was widespread concern that the mismatched fiscal and monetary policies could lead eventually to a full-scale industrial collapse. The frightening scenario for Depression went like this: the economy would stage a mild recovery from the recession in the summer of 1982 but high interest rates would continue because of the horrendous federal deficits. The high interest rates would stall out the new recovery and scores of industrial firms, already over-extended on credit and short of cash from the preceding recession, would be unable to clean up their balance sheets. The next recession would finish them. If large and, presumably, productive enterprises went "belly up," this might produce a cascade of bankruptcies across the economy, as nervous banks began to cut their losses and call in corporate loans. The fears proved to be groundless but never quite went away. The recovery was at first much stronger than expected, but the vigor lasted only eighteen months (long enough to boost Reagan's popularity for the 1984 campaign). After that, the economy stagnated, growing too slowly to reduce unemployment to normal levels, while interest rates remained unusually high.

Henry Kaufman of Salomon Brothers, whose warnings had disturbed Stockman the year before, was even more ominous in his public predictions in the spring of 1982. Kaufman urged Congress to reduce the federal deficits drastically and urged the Federal Reserve Board to modify its monetary policy, lest something dire occur to the national economic fabric.

"We are in an unusual time," Kaufman said in a television appearance. "We are not in a typical cyclical period. We're in a period in which our financial system has become more fragile. For the last three to four years, we have tried to stage a new economic recovery which would be sustainable, and we have failed.

"We have extraordinarily high interest rates today in the United States. We have some institutions that are convalescing. We have certain sectors of the economy that are exceptionally weak. And therefore we must do things that are extraordinary, that are different, that to some extent are painful.

"I am not a political person. I don't know what the political aspects of this tend to suggest. From an economic viewpoint, this is not the time to express strong political dogmas. This is the time to have reconciliation and a degree of certainty in governmental operations that we haven't had before."

Meanwhile, the "supply-side" school, including the *Wall Street Journal*'s editorial writers, kept the faith. The original blueprint for tax-cuts, they complained, had been watered down and delayed in the process of enactment. Instead of a three-year 30 percent reduction, effective January 1, 1981, Congress had cut only 25 percent and postponed its first round to October 1, 1981. Some "supply-siders," drawing upon their classical origins, complained that the monetary control from the Federal Reserve Board was erratic and that the full theory would work only if the United States returned to the gold standard for monetary stability. More to the point, they complained that the tax-cutting policies hadn't been refuted by events—they simply had not been given enough time to work. The era of economic growth would begin, once the recession was over, and the skeptics would see.

In any case, the political community, especially orthodox Republicans in Congress, lost all patience with the theoretical promises from the supply-siders. Indeed, listening to the grim warnings from Volcker and the Brookings economists and Wall Street, the congressional leadership went into a kind of irregular panic of activity, trying to devise a gross package of tax increases and budget reductions, including in defense-spending, which would reverse the lines on the budget chart again. They had no hope of actually balancing a federal budget in the next four or five years; they would settle for restoring the old trendline in which spending and revenue lines were converging, not growing farther apart. When the congressional leadership's search for a grand compromise collapsed in late April, everyone knew they faced a hard summer of political battles over who would pay for last summer's mistakes, with no certain prospect that they could agree on any real solutions before the biennial congressional elections in November.

By that point, the public debate over economic policy seemed totally confused: the participants were not sure whether to follow old orthodoxy or new. The disappointed "supply-siders" pointed out—correctly—that Congress in its new obsession with deficits was ignoring the fundamentals of Keynesian "demand-side" fiscal management. In the midst of recession, the desire to shrink the deficits would have the perverse consequence of taking more money out of the private economy, dampening consumer spending further by raising taxes or reducing federal entitlements like Social Security. It did seem backwards. Furthermore, after all the other bewildering events, no one could be absolutely certain that shrinking the projected deficits would really produce the desired result—lowered interest rates. Congress proceeded into the struggle anyway, knowing only that it had to do something.

In hindsight, one can make a plausible case that the dislocations caused by the Reagan economic policy were largely avoidable—that the President and his advisers and the Congress were captivated by a wrong idea or, at least, a sound idea that came along at the wrong time. In addition to the contradictory cures prescribed by the "supply-side" policies, there may also have been a deeper flaw in the "supply-side" diagnosis of what was wrong with the American economy. There are any number of alternative explanations about why the U.S. economy limped through a decade of inflation and stagnation, its productive growth

stalled out, and the competing explanations do not place all
the blame on the government in Washington. One principal source of inflation, for instance, was hardly a secret—
the quadrupling of oil prices, leapfrogging with spiralling
food prices. The inflationary impact from these basic commodities rippled through the cost and profit of every economic enterprise, not to mention every worker's wages
and real purchasing power. During the same period, the
U.S. job economy was absorbing an historic flood of new
workers—the young people coming of age from the "baby
boom," and mature women entering the job market for the
first time. The number of entry-level jobs increased enor-
mously to accommodate this influx and the overall effect
was lowered productivity, since new and inexperienced
workers are normally less productive and therefore pull
down the average. At the same time, America's basic
industrial sectors, from steel to automobiles, were under-
going their own individual traumas, competing with new
and more efficient international rivals and confronting the
fact that their own plants and production methods had
grown old, out-of-date. Some economists believed these
underlying causes contributed as much, perhaps more, to
the decade of economic disorder than the marginal tax
rates or even the size of federal deficits. The point is that
these were large and historic changes that government
action might influence but not fully control.

If that was the case, a new administration coming to
office in 1981 might well have been cheered by the good
news for the future. The world's economy was adjusting
successfully to the reality of higher oil prices; conservation
by industry and consumers had dampened demand for oil
dramatically and the resulting international surplus was
softening prices. At the least, there would be a lengthy
breathing spell for everyone before another round of oil
price escalation. The demographics of the workforce were

changing, too, in positive ways: the floodtide of new young workers had crested by 1981 and was beginning to decline. One could predict a steady improvement in U.S. productivity rates (as well as employment prospects for young people) as the pool of workers grew older, more experienced and more efficient. Finally, while the decline of basic industrial sectors continued and, in some cases, was probably irreversible, this lost economic activity—both profits and jobs—was being replaced by new sectors built around new technologies. In any case, it wouldn't make much sense to pour new capital into expanding the American steel industry, for instance, when the world already had a gross overcapacity for steel production, well in excess of the world's demand for steel products. If these premises were correct, then the new administration might have opted for a more orthodox mix of policies, policies which gently encouraged the positive trends or at least kept the government from damaging them.

Given these deep-seated problems, the Reagan economic policy did nothing to improve prospects and may have made things worse. Despite the supposed benefits of reduced inflation, American industry did not restore healthy growth in productivity, the key barometer for future prosperity. Savings and investment did not increase as the supply-siders had promised; personal and corporate debt soared. To offset the huge deficits, the Federal Reserve and the financial markets kept interest rates at extraordinarily high levels, dampening the expansion and shifting wealth regressively from debtors to creditors. Overall, the economic growth rate under Ronald Reagan was markedly slower than in the 1970s under Jimmy Carter and his predecessors. The rhetoric of miraculous results simply did not match the facts.

The same paradox of power returns in another form, the same confusion about the impact of government. The conservative reformers, from Ronald Reagan to the most millennial "supply-siders," were all convinced that the federal government was the engine of economic disorder—the only engine that mattered to them—just as Stockman believed, in the realm of special-interest programs, that the "permanent government" itself created the appetite for federal largesse, not the myriad constituencies of citizens and businesses who received it. Thus, in a peculiar way, conservatives are apt to see the federal government as more awesome in its impact on society than old-fashioned liberals do. It does sound strange, the idea that conservatives in their hostility to Washington should assign it greater importance in the scheme of things than it actually deserves. But the obsession of conservative ideologues is like a negative mirror of the stereotypical hubris of liberals: one believes the central government can accomplish everything good in life and the other believes the central government has already caused everything dreadful. From either side of the ideological divide, this illusion is seductive for the participants because both sides struggle in the same contest for political hegemony. If a President and his party have captured control of the government, it is a bit disappointing to be told that the government cannot influence or even mediate every facet of American life. Conservative reformers wish to make history, too, by their own governmental decisions, and they do not want to be told that history has its own deep forces larger than governments. If an activist President like Ronald Reagan cannot control the deeper tides of history, then he will control what he can—the policies of government—and hope that these produce the future that he promised. Sometimes, of course, they will. And sometimes, a President will try to fix things which aren't even broken.

IV.
Trapped by the Seasons

By the summer of 1982, less than a year after his great legislative triumphs, the decline of Ronald Reagan's presidential authority was tangible, visible to all. By the summer of 1983, when unemployment peaked and began subsiding, Reagan's popular standing began improving again. It rose steadily throughout 1984 and continued strong into his second term. Yet his presidency had been changed, particularly in terms of setting fiscal policy for the government. His authority over the federal budget—the central document of policy-making—was never restored to its original level. He was immensely popular as a political figure but no longer so formidable as a leader. Neither the Congress nor the general public were willing to accept his priorities for spending. Ronald Reagan sent four successive budgets to Capitol Hill and each one was declared "dead on arrival."

The political seasons are fickle and brief and occasionally cruel. This is a familiar story for the modern American presidency, a recurring event, it seems. Each new leader marshals public support for his ideas, assaults the opposition barricades and perhaps triumphs—only to fall back defeated, trapped by competing realities or undone by the hubris of his own policies. The forward-looking visions of recent Presidents each seemed compelling in one season and ludicrously flawed in the next. When this contradiction occurs, some critics will reexamine the President's personality and discover the reasons. Others will bemoan the inconstancy of the public and propose institutional reforms which would insulate the presidency from the ill winds of changing opinion. Neither critique is likely to change much of anything. Americans, after all, will continue to elect fallible human beings as President and, in this era of populist cynicism about government, the proposals for a six-year term for the President or parliamentary discipline to enforce congressional loyalty are exceedingly remote.

The casebook before us suggests the outlines of other explanations, modest insights that at least describe what is happening to modern Presidents. To summarize crudely, it comes down to this: Presidents are still using old magic in an age when the new magic is swift and more powerful. They predict good weather and a bountiful harvest for the future, then lose control of the seasons. They propose grand new ideas, then lose sight of their substance. They begin by promising miracles, then end up begging for patience. Along the way, faced with the tactical necessities of the political struggle, they also tell lies. Perhaps they hope the lies will turn out to be true or, at least, that the truth will not catch up with them. In the modern age, it nearly always does.

We elect a powerful new king and, each time, we discover he really resembles the Wizard of Oz. This depressing condition of the presidency does not suggest that a modern leader must learn to operate without the uses of myth and mystery that leaders have always invoked; I think that is a permanent condition of human society which even American democracy, with all of its rationalist pretensions, cannot repeal. It does seem relevant to observe, however, that Ronald Reagan's "mistakes" of leadership, once they are stripped of personal and ideological peculiarities, were not so different from Jimmy Carter's mistakes or Nixon's or Johnson's. Each of those Presidents operated with an inflated sense of his own authority, a conception of presidential authority which political Washington reinforces in its daily behavior but which ultimately fails the tests of reality. Each President, one can argue, sets himself up for failure and waits for events to fulfill the tragic prophecy.

Reagan, one has to add, indulged in the old magic more shamelessly than some of the others. His vision invoked a very simple idea for this complex world, the idea of returning nostalgically to an age of laissez-faire conservatism. This resonated powerfully with the collective anti-government sentiments of the general public and, indeed, he swept along the center of conventional political opinion. Ordinary congressmen and senators who were interested in their own practical survival as elected officials thought they saw deeper currents in Reagan's stunning election victory. If Reagan was the future, then they had better get on board. Looking back on the legislative battles of 1981, one can see that the new President had won the basic argument even before the first roll call. The Democratic opposition and the moderate Republicans, despite their personal distaste for Reagan and his ideology, had already accepted the soundness of his general premises. The Democratic alternative was political mimickry; it also would cut taxes drastically and shrink the domestic budget and increase defense-spending. For the working politicians, Reagan's vision had an aura of inevitability.

So the new President began with enormous political capital and gradually he squandered it. As one considers how this happened, the elements of Reagan's presidential behavior are recognizable because similar qualities were seen in his predecessors, who dealt in different circumstances with different kinds of problems.

First, from the outset, the new President misled the public in fundamental ways. In addition to his grandiose claims for the "supply-side" tax reductions, Reagan misstated the true dimensions of what his economic recovery program would require in terms of personal sacrifice from the public. The longer he continued to do this, the more it looked like deliberate deception. To cite the grossest example, Reagan promised repeatedly that the so-called "safety net" programs, including Social Security and Medicare, would be off limits to his budget-cutting. This was clever in tactical terms because it reassured a major middle-class constituency, the elderly, and finessed the volatile question of how to reform those entitlement programs. But Reagan did intend to cut those programs, probably from the start. Anyone who studied the administration's budget projections could see that there was literally no way for him to reach his other goals—increased defense-spending, tax reduction, a balanced budget—without trying to cut the major entitlement programs. Reagan, one assumes, was not so opaque to his own proposals that he did not understand this. Soon enough, he did try, only to back away when the elderly arose in wrath. A year later, he was still gingerly fencing with the objective, trying to accomplish a reduction without seeming to sponsor it.

Leadership must be "visible and legible" to maintain authority, according to Richard Sennett's brilliant essay "Authority." Sennett was describing lines of authority in large bureaucratic organizations, but presumably the same rule would apply to a political leader drawing authority from the citizens of a large and complicated nation. If a President does not state clearly what he will require of his followers, sooner or later they will hold him accountable for misleading them. Reagan's promises, of course, were no more grandiose than what Lyndon Johnson had promised—an end to poverty in America—or more deceptive than Richard Nixon's pledge to end the war in Indochina.

And Reagan's erratic positions on sacrificing Social Security were reminiscent of Jimmy Carter's on energy policy. The point, of course, is that each President undermined his own authority.

Ronald Reagan's obligation to be frank was greater than his predecessors'. Reagan really did propose a fundamental departure from the past. He was attempting, as Stockman said, to alter a direction of government that had endured for more than twenty years, to shift the spending priorities and to begin the actual shrinkage of government. Whether this was a wise goal or a foolish one, it could hardly be accomplished by sleight-of-hand. Something so fundamental required fundamental argument in its behalf, a clear explanation of the consequences and the risks. Instead, Reagan hid behind artful sophistry. The government would be scaled back merely by eliminating "waste, fraud, and abuse," not by directly challenging the perquisites and privileges of citizen groups. Reagan's own advisers understood perfectly well that this ducked the issue. In time, the public figured it out, too.

In hard political terms, Reagan and his advisers misunderstood the seasons. Putting aside the question of whether entitlement reductions were wise or necessary, if Reagan was going to propose them, he should have done so at the very start, when his own power to persuade and rally public support was at its maximum. As former congressman Stockman understood, any dramatic and painful choices about Social Security would probably have to be made in 1981 because 1982 was an election year. Postponement would only harden the resistance. As it was, Reagan proposed to Congress that it do the easiest part first—cutting taxes—and put off the most painful issues until later. The administration did, of course, stipulate with the "magic asterisk" that further budget reductions would have to follow in the ensuing years, but this tactic merely permitted their collaborators in Congress to deceive themselves, too. When finally the issue of entitlement reductions was no longer avoidable, Congress was deep into its reelection campaign and neither party was anxious to take the blame. Thus, a major area of budget reform was lost because the President had chosen to approach it obliquely instead of directly and, yes, honestly.

Of course, Presidents should tell the truth, but my point is slightly more complicated than that. Politicians, like other human beings, do dissemble and I do not naïvely yearn for a new generation of politicians who will only speak the truth. What Presidents need to understand, however, is that the complexity of events and the response mechanisms available to ordinary citizens have greatly reduced the forebearance for deception. One season's decisions, based on false premises, become intricately embedded in the next season's choices and, despite dramatic gestures and rhetoric, the underlying facts come back with brutal directness to confront the leader with last season's lies. Moreover, the very complexity of the political issues and the awesome size of modern institutions, especially the federal government, already engender popular suspicions about what's really going on. Yet successive Presidents addressed this generalized public skepticism with millennial language that comes back to haunt them. In the global village, there is no place to hide.

Second, the Reagan program was inevitably transformed by the process of enactment itself. As Stockman recounted so vividly, the tax and budget proposals proceeded through an unseemly gauntlet of compromise and trading. At the end, the revenue losses were much larger than anyone had proposed at the White House and the budget savings were smaller. Skeptical economists had assumed the congressional process would moderate Reagan's program. Instead, it exaggerated its damaging effects. In addition, odious subsidy programs were tacked on as extra baggage, needed to win the "marginal votes" for passage, which were directly contradictory to the original vision Reagan had launched. The government would get off some citizens' backs, but not others. The federal largesse would be ended for certain classes of citizens, but enlarged for others. The President did not object. Tactical choices again weakened the authority of what he was promising.

This, too, is hardly a new phenomenon of government. Every idea which enters the legislative process faces the same risks, particularly any radical departure from the status quo which promises a pure vision of reform. For many seasons, liberal reformers experienced the same disappointment, watching their proposals lose their original integrity as they moved from the theoretical realm into the messy arena where a majority rules and each needed vote may extract a concession. When Lyndon Johnson's Great Society programs were enacted in the 1960s, despite his legendary political acumen and the lopsided Democratic majorities in Congress, many programs were transformed in this manner. Typically, a new social program was test-marketed as a "demonstration project," found to be effective, then submitted as a general legislation to serve the entire nation. Again and again, in education and health, welfare and job-training, the original design was altered in the congressional enactment, watered down or transformed into a new version of pork barrel. The legislated program became something quite different from the original premise. This helped explain why so many of those social programs seemed to fail on large-scale application, despite their success on small-scale tests. Usually, the political leader, whether it is Lyndon Johnson or Ronald Reagan, will settle for what he can get and what he wants to get is a victory for his program, whatever the price of compromise.

The process of compromise is the legislative process, of course; the necessities of messy trading are both the permanent curse and the saving grace of representative democracy. This is a reality not likely to change much, from season to season. Yet each President pretends that his ideas are exempt from corruption. Any new political idea, whether it is visionary laissez-faire conservatism or visionary welfare liberalism, might be subjected to this stern test: the new idea can be said to lack substance, regardless of its theoretical elegance, until its advocates can plausibly chart its course through the political arena in a manner that will not destroy its original integrity. A great many legislative inventions enacted under modern Presidents of both parties would not pass that test. And many participants in government would object that the standard is too purist. In season and out, liberal legislators and conservatives practice a kind of incrementalism, settling for a modest beginning for their ideas, a foot-in-the-door which perhaps can be improved upon next year or the year after. Programs are therefore begun with inadequate funding which ensures their failure; laws are written that no one expects to be fully enforced. The cumulative effect, I think, is to undermine the effectiveness of government. Indeed, it depreciates the very idea of government as an institution which makes certain guarantees to citizens and keeps them, which enacts laws and upholds them. The Reagan Administration has now made its contribution to this legacy because, like other Presidents before him, Reagan could not say "no" to his own initiatives.

Finally, trapped in the changing seasons, a President begins to betray his own mythology or abandons it in search of a new vision that may restore his declining authority. In this regard, Reagan has clearly been more loyal to his own fundamentals than his predecessors were. Jimmy Carter alternated the direction of both his foreign policy and his economic management to accommodate each new event, and events treated him badly. Richard

Nixon switched abruptly from free-market conservative to the only modern President to enforce wage and price controls. In these terms, Reagan has been a more stable leader. He compromised on his budget and taxation only under intense pressure from his own party, knowing perhaps that a President may never recover once he has yielded his basic principles. Still, judging from the actions of his own advisers and the independent initiatives taken by congressional Republicans, Reagan would have to give more ground before the budget crisis was resolved.

Many of the active proposals in Congress directly offended the laissez-faire doctrine which Reagan had espoused. Republicans, for instance, wanted a new tax on imported oil, partly to raise revenue and partly to support the sagging prices of domestic oil. This was only a year after Reagan had completed the decontrol of oil prices and restored the "magic of the free marketplace." Yet he remained silent. Other conservatives were preparing a legislative bail-out for the housing industry, a $5 billion program to subsidize interest rates on home mortgages. Still others were enacting a major new job-training program to partially replace what Reagan had abolished the year before. Perhaps, as Stockman had said, there were no "real conservatives" in Congress.

Would the President acquiesce in these interventionist initiatives? If he did, each would take something more away from the legitimacy of his original myth. If he balked, however, he might also lose control, encouraging Congress to believe that he was blind to present realities. That, of course, was always the problem with Reagan's vision of the future. It looked backward in time and hoped to recreate the past. If the laissez-faire vision was tattered, it was partly because its sponsors had never adequately calculated how they could sustain it from one season to the next, holding back the natural activist forces of the political process which wish to deal with problems of the here and now.

How might a successful President address the future? He could begin by emphasizing in his public promises what every modern President has had to learn in private frustration: that the future guarantees only complexity and abrupt changes. The rest is hope and inspiration. That one season of politics decides nothing conclusively. That one President may be able to alter the direction of events without necessarily controlling them.

A President might announce as his new dogma what ought to be obvious from recent history; namely, that he can see the future but dimly. He is guided by faith and principle, and he does have a plan but, in time, as events unfold, he will probably see things differently. He will probably have to change his plan, perhaps even seek compromise with his opponents. He will try to guide the nation where he thinks it should go, but life is full of uncertainty and he is as fallible as other citizens. Politicians shrink from this mushy talk, of course; the people want clear answers and they try to provide them. But that mode of leadership doesn't work as well as it once did. Perhaps there is a useful source of mystery in humility, if a politician handles it right. Perhaps there is a modern version of authority to be derived from acknowledging the limits of one's power.

Ronald Reagan, one could say, had no reason to compromise further. He had already accomplished much of what he came to Washington to do: launching the rearming of America and putting a noose around the size of the federal government. This fulfilled his personal vision, the speech he had been making for twenty years. Now he could sit back and watch others scramble for remedies to the staggering deficits he had produced. This, too, however, was a form of forfeiture. The mythology of shrinking the government had created practical political problems, real dislocations which affected real people. To this, the President had no solutions to offer, beyond recommending that they shrink it some more. That was last year's magic, and it had lost its charm.

V.

Reassuring Anarchy

When David Stockman revealed with disarming candor that "none of us really understands what's going on with all these numbers," many were shocked and even frightened. The revelation that the basic budget numbers of the federal government were not altogether reliable alarmed many of his fellow politicians who had no right to be alarmed. Either they were hypocritical or remarkably inattentive. Stockman's account of chaotic decision-making at the top also frightened many private citizens, even sophisticated students of government who thought they understood the nature of political deliberations. What was revealed, instead, was a kind of natural anarchy, a helter-skelter sequence of events normally concealed from public view. Is no one in control, even at the highest levels of power? Is that how government really works?

The permanent answer, I am convinced, is yes. A great deal of energy is expended by public officials to convey the opposite impression, the appearance of calm deliberation and decisiveness. The press in its daily coverage contributes to this impression. The tone and structure of the daily news reports inevitably imply a sense of order, even when the details are about calamity. Each day one reads a new prediction or decision in the news from Washington, about the economy or the prospect of war or whatever, and the implicit message is that the government is functioning. Somewhere someone is in charge.

Democratic partisans pretended to be deeply horrified by Stockman's admissions, but any honest reflection by those who served in preceding administrations or who serve now on congressional budget committees would concede that the Reagan administration's internal chaos was not unique, not even extraordinary. That is the experience of government, repeated again and again, of those mortals chosen to manage the complexities of the technocratic state. If one could administer truth serum to the budget directors who served under Johnson, Nixon, Ford, and Carter, they would be compelled to relate similar nightmares of confusion: runaway numbers that refused to conform to their predictions, bad guesses and wishful thinking that shaped major policy decisions, unforeseen events that wiped out their theoretical premises or sometimes rescued them from disasters.

Generally, the memoirs of public servants do not dwell upon the inherent chaos; they emphasize order, too. They talk about how hard everyone worked and how difficult it was to govern. Once in a while, however, a chance revelation of history occurs prematurely and confirms the continuing presence of anarchy within. The Pentagon Papers disclosed, memorandum by memorandum, the haphazard strategy-making which led the nation into Vietnam. The Watergate revelations and the CIA disclosures which followed revealed the same disturbing chaos, not to mention criminal behavior. These accidental portraits of powerful men in action were not ennobling: Presidents and advisers were propelled by panic and paranoia, by the obsessive need to keep up appearances. Johnson's war strategists and Nixon's plumbers were regularly blindsided by unpredicted developments, like Reagan's economic advisers. The response in every instance was to mask the new reality, to pretend either that it had not happened or to invent a new rationale to cover the policies. No one likes to confront the possibility that, as Stockman put it, the "random elements" are out of control. Officers of government, in particular, will struggle to convince their opponents, foreign and domestic, that they really are in charge of events when clearly they are not. These powerful people who run government are, after all, fallible human beings like the rest of us.

But citizens crave a sense of order, too. If the general public does not believe democratic government is functioning in its behalf, then how can it function at all? This question leads some political scientists, those who are more preoccupied with the problems of the governing elite than with the yearnings of popular will, to complain about the occasional disclosures of inner chaos in government. It is not that they deny the haphazard reality revealed by the portraiture, but they think it is unwise to share that gloomy knowledge with the general public. People will only be frightened and lose faith.

By now, it should be obvious that my own convictions run deeply in the opposite direction. I find the anarchy in high places strangely reassuring. I think it is essential knowledge for every American, knowledge that can liberate citizens by assuring them of their own worth in the political process. The core of democratic possibilities lies in the realization by ordinary people that the political elite who decide things, whether it is foreign policy or budget forecasts, are not so different from themselves. Members of the elite have collected specialized knowledge and discovered how to enter the channels of power and influence outcomes. But they react to daily life with the same collection of uncertainties and imponderables that govern the lives of individuals anywhere else in the society.

Powerful elite groups, especially when they operate from

large and remote bureaucracies, will always try to intimidate outsiders with their expertise. The issue of nuclear strategy must be left to the national-security experts. Questions of education must be decided by educators. Matters of economic policy are too dense and complicated for plain citizens to understand. Yet, each time the veil is lifted, ordinary citizens can see for themselves—despite their distance from Washington or their lack of formal knowledge—that expert judgments are no better than their own. They are a mixture of hope and luck and even, sometimes, common sense. Many Americans—perhaps most Americans —have an intuitive sense of this: the remote experts do not have all the answers. All I am suggesting is that their intuition is right.

Given the malaise and confusion which have eroded the foundations of national politics, it requires an act of will to be optimistic about the future. The recurring failure of leaders and the domination of new political technologies undermine faith and citizen participation. Despite the rising levels of income and educational attainment among Americans, which ought to predict greater participation, the electorate has been shrinking as a percentage of adults. Roughly half of the eligible citizens no longer find it worthwhile or necessary to vote in presidential elections. As the audience shrinks, the influence of video images seems to increase—images manufactured by professional consultants and financed by huge pools of campaign money. The presence of special-interest contributions, particularly the millions raised by corporate political-action committees, threatens to dominate the selection of candidates as well as the outcome of election contests, particularly in Congress. From these trends, it is easy enough to construct a dark view of the future. Democracy is in trouble.

I am convinced, nevertheless, that ordinary citizens can act successfully upon their commonsense insights about government. In the future, I believe millions of them will, perhaps forcefully enough to ventilate the closed circle of policymakers and overpower the campaign money supplied by the special interests. What is required is a kind of political reeducation for everyone, a new and wiser sense of both how government and politics really function, and also how easily they can be influenced by outside pressure mobilized by ordinary citizens. Citizens must work their way toward a new political literacy. I hope this volume is helpful in that struggle.

After many years in the news business, I came to the conclusion, independent of the Stockman episode, that there are fundamental flaws in the way the news media package reality and convey it to the general population. Surely these weaknesses contribute in some measure to the malaise and confusion. Americans consume more information about public affairs now than at any previous point in history, yet they do not seem to have gained a deeper understanding of events, much less control over them, from this deluge. How, after all, can an ordinary citizen with only a limited interest really know what's happening? How does the outsider get beyond the politician's rhetoric and see the deeper reality of ongoing events?

He begins, I hope, with healthy skepticism toward all grand claims made in the political arena. He applies his own common sense to all propositions, particularly ones which suggest magical solutions to enduring problems. He does not rely on experts. He asks himself: does this make sense? He examines his own impulses: am I voting for an empty sentiment from the past or for a plausible vision of the future? Until Americans get those questions straight in their own heads, they will continue to be deluded by TV performers of one variety or another. Presiding over the U.S. government is not like starring in a television series. The networks cannot cancel a President when his ratings decline. A viewer cannot switch channels if his hero begins to falter. The President was chosen for four years, not one season, and his promises, as well as his performance, should be judged on that basis.

As voters become wiser, however, they are still dependent on the images and information with which the news media provide them. The press, I think, has to reinvent its definitions of news, just as political candidates have to redefine the mystery of leadership. The present news values place an extraordinary premium on essentially contradictory elements: the immediacy of what happened yesterday and the prophecy of what will happen in the distant future. On many days, these two elements will be merged and the dominant "news" will consist almost entirely of predictions made yesterday about what might happen in the future. I do not expect news organizations to abandon those values entirely, but it ought to be obvious that their emphasis leaves readers with a rather incoherent sense of time and continuity. In the daily news, there is no "past," only today and the far-off tomorrow. A daily newspaper or the evening TV news broadcast is not likely to conclude that "today" or "yesterday" are less compelling than "last month" or "last year." After all, they are in the business of *daily* news. But it is surely possible to reimagine how stories are to be told and what is to be the most important content.

The values slighted are the ones probably most valuable to the consumer: context and comprehension. While the best reporters and editors do care about them, the reigning conventions of the news business do not. The governing impulse is to simplify and startle. The historic legacy of modern media tells the practitioners that this is what the audience craves. But the modern deluge of information has changed the audience, I believe, in ways that the conventional news organizations simply do not recognize. People seem to "know" everything now—hearing the same news bulletins repeated around the clock—but they seem to understand precious little of what's really going on. That is what they crave—understanding.

The business of news ought to take responsibility for what the consumers of news understand. If that sounds obvious, it is really a radical proposition for news organizations. They see themselves as neutral conveyors, responsible only for delivering the startling facts as they occur. To go further would require the objective journalist to tread beyond the safe limits of what is knowable from daily reporting into the analytical realm where the reporter is obligated to try to make sense of things for the reader. It would force the reporter to question the implicit limitations he has accepted in his transactions with public officials. It would challenge the comfortable arrangements of symbiosis and depreciate the closed system that exists between press and politicians. The system sustains itself on mutual needs: a politician who learns that the press will only treat simplistic rhetoric as news will learn how to fill that need—or else find himself shut out of the news columns. Reporters who complain privately about political demagoguery and distortion usually lack the freedom to call it that in print.

In short, I question the narrow rules of objectivity which govern news judgments and inhibit the news media from truly describing the full reality before them. As an editor, I was acutely aware of the criticism aroused when newspapers strayed beyond those limits. Readers who long for comprehension will nevertheless complain about analytical stories which offend their version of the truth. They will denounce the reporting as "slanted" and admonish the newspaper to simply report the facts without embellishment. Mostly, this is what newspapers do, with unsatisfactory results.

The best new journalism will take the risks and try to go deeper—not self-indulgently or for partisan advantage—but to share more fully with the reader or TV viewer what the reporters themselves understand to be happening. Often the reporters will be wrong. They will see events through distorted lenses. They will not always be able to dig to the deeper level of reality. Still, I think the audience will understand more if they try to explain more and startle less. Instead of endlessly asking what's going to happen next, the news media ought to devote more energy to a different question: what did happen really? The more that question is asked, the more public officials will be compelled to provide honest answers. Newspapers and TV will discover that the past can be as startling as the present and the future.

Beyond the influence of the news media, however, citizens can act upon their own insights about politics, and they do. The old magic still works to win elections—especially when the new leader promises a bountiful harvest without any rain—but a growing number of citizens have come to recognize the hollowness of these promises. The possibility of genuine democracy has, in fact, atrophied in the last generation. As more and more alienated citizens conclude that participation is not efficacious, even at the simplest level of voting, the center of political decisions tilts further right, for both Democratic and Republican candidates. In Reagan's famous landslide of 1980, when America was supposedly turning to conservative reform, barely half of the adult citizens actually voted. In his celebrated triumph of 1984, the turnout improved, but only slightly. The result is an inevitable distortion of representation and influence. Money talks in politics and always has, but it speaks with more force when huge pools of ordinary citizens give up on the potential of political action.

The deterioration of the two parties and the gravitational pull toward the concerns of upper-income voters and institutions will likely get worse before there is any genuine reversal of the democratic decay. In the short run, politicians do what they need to do in order to win, regardless of their ideological preferences. If that means playing to the galleries where the upper-middle-class sits and currying approval (and campaign contributions) from corporate lobbies, then most will pursue these opportunities. The retreat from broader interests will probably continue, effectively leaving a large segment of the American population unrepresented.

In time, this creates an opening for new politics, even new parties, if they are willing to say aloud what the two major parties are afraid to espouse. A new splinter politician in the Midwest might challenge the prevailing wisdom of farm economics and promise a debt moratorium for the failing farmers in Iowa or Nebraska. Established politicians would dismiss that as irresponsible, yet it speaks directly to the disaster affecting millions across the farm belt. If one eccentric voice succeeds, actually wins an election against the overwhelming advantages held by the established parties, then others will surely try to do the same. The conventional view would be that this process, if it takes hold, is destabilizing for government, sowing chaos and stalemate. My own view, obviously, is that it would be profoundly invigorating—forcing Democrats and Republicans to confront the real grievances they do not now represent.

The splintering of party politics naturally frightens orthodox politicians and political scientists, but it is a very old tradition in American politics, a development which usually presages fundamental change. If one is satisfied with the status quo, that thought is alarming. But clearly most Americans are not satisfied and the idea of splinter parties ought to be regarded as healthy competition, forcing the major parties and their presidential candidates to change or perish.

In the meantime, citizens have also discovered that they do not have to wait for the next election to be effective in politics. The knowledge that the inner circle of policymakers is a world of chaos and fallibility ought to stimulate more direct action by citizens, encouraging them to assert their own claims on the public agenda and to force open the closed processes of decision-making. This is already happening, of course, and most politicians dread it. They describe the intruders derisively as "single-interest groups" but the idea of popular participation is as old as democracy. In recent years, irregular groups of citizens from left, right, and center have pushed their way into the action, discovering that they, too, can mobilize popular support by working outside the established channels of power. If this story of the Reagan Administration suggests any single point worth remembering, I think it is this: the established channels of remote political power are much more vulnerable to citizen influence than either the system or the citizenry appreciate. It is, after all, an accidental process, subject to accidental events and the influence of new ideas and personalities. Given the general dissatisfaction with the status quo, I think American politics resembles a vast vacuum, waiting to be filled by those who are bold and energetic and, yes, lucky enough to try.

This much is clear: despite the inequalities of wealth and status, despite the concentrated power of corporate America, the political system does react swiftly to new intruders, even if it resents their presence. The New Right groups and the Moral Majority are the latest examples of this irregular action. Whatever else one may say about their values and objectives, those new movements are populist in intent, if not in origin. They mean to empower ordinary citizens, the middle-class and lower-middle-class, who feel the government is ignoring their desires for society. To mobilize support, however, they employ the most modern techniques—television evangelism and computer-run fundraising by mail. As a political organism, the New Right was actually born in Washington among young conservatives who were consciously imitating the organizational techniques developed by earlier citizen movements of the left—the consumer and environmental groups, the Common Cause reformers, the campaign to end the war in Vietnam. All of those citizen campaigns were, of course, drawing their inspiration from the civil rights movement which invented most of the modern methods for accomplishing important political goals outside the regular electoral process.

Each of these movements produced fundamental change and reached some of their objectives. Their weaknesses, however, have been reflected in recent events, as the Reagan Administration has proceeded to undo many of the earlier victories. The conservative thrust produced its own reaction, however. Reagan's indifference to arms control restimulated the citizens' movement for nuclear sanity and the President was compelled to moderate his rhetoric and at least create the impression that he too believed in arms reduction. The environmental movement, thanks to the threat of James Watt and other Reagan appointees, managed to stalemate nearly every effort to dilute environmental regulations. The war is not over, but the "outsiders" are winning more battles than they are losing.

The question, however, is whether the next era of citizen action can move beyond its own limitations in the past. As long as citizens mobilize around fairly narrow objectives, they will find that the permanent political apparatus reacts to their pressures, but that many of their victories are also perishable, unless they are able to impose permanent change on the behavior of the dominant institutions themselves. The singlemindedness which makes them effective crusades also makes them vulnerable, in time, to erosion and neglect, once the popular pressure has subsided. This has always been the frailty of citizen movements and it suggests that, in order to produce deeper changes, the new populists must borrow from the old populists and develop a broader critique of government and politics. This means addressing the fundamental issues of government power—taxation, war and peace, subsidy, and security—and the social realities of class and inequality implicit in those policies. I do not expect that this will produce popular upheaval, but I do think it has the modest potential to force new ideas upon the status quo. The community of government now decides those questions largely by debating with itself, the closed conversation among government technocrats and existing interest groups, a dialogue only rarely interrupted by popular expressions of dissent. Naturally, this intrusion into fundamentals would make life even messier for the governing elite, but those circles need the competition of outside ideas and provocative claims from unrecognized citizens. Small-d democracy is messy and chaotic by nature, but it also can be creative. If people genuinely accept the legitimacy of the outcomes, it can produce a shared sense of order.

In any case, the absolute power of Washington is less than it seems, certainly less than the permanent participants of Washington believe it to be. In stressing that point throughout this volume, I am not making an ideological choice about big government versus small government or laissez-faire conservatism versus welfare-state liberalism. I am merely emphasizing a broader reality about the complexity of American society and how it functions.

Washington is not the capital of everything. That may be self-evident to most Americans, but the point gets easily lost by the governing elite, liberal and conservative. Washington is the capital of government, but its persuasions and commandments compete with decisions from other capitals. New York City is the capital of finance, among other things, and Wall Street may veto the wishes of a President if those wishes do not make economic sense to investment analysts. Houston is the capital of oil and the decisions of oil can bring down governments or launch foreign wars. Los Angeles is the capital of entertainment, which manufactures other myths for the citizens to consume; perhaps more engaging myths than the ones which mere politicians have to offer. Detroit was the capital of heavy industry; its choices determined the future health of American manufacturing. But perhaps that capital has moved now to Silicon Valley and Route 128, where private decisions will guide the nation's commerce in information technology. And where exactly is the capital of agriculture? In many places; California, Iowa, Georgia, depending on the commodity. The point is that each capital of economic activity, wherever one fixes it on the map, possesses its own version of political power, the ability to check and counter what the political government in Washington has proclaimed. If one looks at American politics in this more fluid sense, the central government in Washington does not look so awesome. Indeed, in many realms, it is quite weak. It promises and implores, but dares not command. It sets rules for lawful behavior, then negotiates with rule-breakers. It imagines that symbolic gestures will persuade, but lacks the strength or courage to compel.

Conservatives, as I have said, seem as confused about this as liberals. Both have inherited the same mythology of modern government and the modern presidency, and the daily action of Washington constantly reinforces their illusion of presiding over every important outcome. This contributes to the confused uses of power which have become the hallmark of modern Presidents, the confusion of abstract purposes with concrete actions. Within constitutional limitations, the government does have extraordinary and tangible powers. It collects taxes and sends out money to eligible citizens. It can order a factory to stop dumping poisons in the river. Or it can subsidize the growth of one industry while allowing another to decline. It can make wars, conscript citizens to fight, bomb the enemy. All these are real uses of real power. All will produce tangible effects. They should not be employed as gestures of good intent or as exhortations to faith. If the government chooses to control outcomes, it has to do it by controlling these uses of power. Like Presidents, government, too, must be "visible and legible."

Finally, if these confusions surrounding government were to disappear abruptly, the effect would also be liberating for the politicians and technocrats who operate within the permanent anarchy. The continuing confusion will always be frustrating. But they would at least be relieved of that constant burden of denial and concealment. Even in politics, confronting reality rather than hiding from it may prove to be, not merely right, but also smart.

Appendixes

Avoiding a GOP Economic Dunkirk

BY DAVID STOCKMAN
DECEMBER, 1980

Excerpts from a Speech to the New York Stock Exchange Directors

BY DAVID STOCKMAN
JUNE, 1985

I.
THE GATHERING STORM

The momentum of short-run economic, financial, and budget forces is creating the conditions for an economic Dunkirk during the first twenty-four months of the Reagan Administration. These major factors threaten:

1) A Second 1980 Credit Crunch

By year end bank rates are likely to hit the 15–17 percent range, causing further deterioration in long-term capital markets for bonds and equities, a renewed consumer spending slowdown, and intensified uncertainty throughout financial markets.

There are a number of potential contributory forces. The most important is the fact that the Fed [Federal Reserve Board] has been substantially overshooting its 1980 money supply growth goals ever since mid-summer. Were Volcker to attempt to use the interregnum to impose the severe constraint necessary to get back on track, MI-B, for example, would have to be held to essentially a *zero growth rate* for the remainder of the year to fall within the 6.5 percent upper target for 1980.

In addition, the Treasury will impose massive financing requirements on the market through January 1, including about $100 billion in refinancing and potentially $25–28 billion in new cash requirements at current budget operating levels (fourth quarter). While private credit requirements are likely to soften in response to the emerging slowdown in housing, durables, and other real sectors, year-end seasonal borrowing requirements are still likely to be heavy.

In all, President Reagan will inherit thoroughly disordered credit and capital markets, punishingly high interest rates, and a hair-trigger market psychology poised to respond strongly to early economic policy signals in either favorable or unfavorable ways.

The preeminent danger is that an initial economic policy package that includes the tax cuts but does not contain *decisive, credible elements* on matters of outlay control, future budget authority reduction, and a believable plan for curtailing the federal government's massive direct and indirect credit absorption will generate pervasive expectations of a continuing *"Reagan inflation."* Such a development would almost ensure that high interest rates would hang over the economy well into the first year, deadening housing and durables markets and thwarting the industrial capital spending boom required to propel sustained economic growth. Thus, Thatcherization can only be avoided if the initial economic policy package simultaneously spurs the output side of the economy and also elicits a swift downward revision of inflationary expectations in the financial markets.

2) A Double-Dip Recession in Early 1981

This is now at least a 50 percent possibility given emerging conditions in the financial markets and gathering evidence from the output side of the economy. Stagnant or declining real GNP [Gross National Product] growth in the first two quarters would generate staggering political and policy challenges. These include a further worsening of an already dismal budget posture (see below) and a profusion of "quick fix" remedies for various "wounded" sectors of the economy. The latter would include intense pressure for formal or informal auto import restraints, activation of Brooke-Cranston or similar costly housing bail-outs, maintenance of current excessive CETA employment levels, accelerated draw-down of various lending and grant aids under SBA, EDA, and FmHA, a further thirteen week extension of federal unemployment benefits, etc. Obviously, the intense political pressures for many of these quick fix aids will distract from the Reagan program on the economic fundamentals (supply-side tax-cuts, regulatory reform, and firm long-term fiscal discipline) and threaten to lock in budget costs and policy initiatives that are out of step with the basic policy thrust.

There is a further danger; the federal budget has now become an automatic *"coast-to-coast soup line"* that dispenses remedial aid with almost reckless abandon, converting the traditional notion of automatic stabilizers into multitudinous outlay spasms throughout the budget. For instance, the estimates for FY 81 [Fiscal Year 1981, ending October 1, 1981] trade adjustment assistance have exploded from $400 million in the spring to $2.5 billion as of November, and the summer drought will cause SBA emergency farm loan aid to surge by $1.1 billion above planned levels.

For these reasons, the first hard look at the unvarnished FY 81 and 82 budget posture by our own OMB people is likely to elicit coronary contractions among some, and produce an intense polarization between supply-side tax-cutters and the more fiscally orthodox. An internecine struggle over deferral or temporary abandonment of the tax program could ensue. The result would be a severe demoralization and fractionalization of GOP ranks and an erosion of our capacity to govern successfully and revive the economy before November 1982.

3) Federal Budget and Credit Hemorrhage

The latest estimates place FY 81 outlays at nearly $650 billion. That represents a *$20 billion* outlay growth since the August estimates; a *$36 billion* growth since the First Budget Resolution passed in June; an outlay level *$73 billion* above FY *80;* and a *$157 billion growth* since the books closed on FY 79 just thirteen months ago.

The table below illustrates the full dimension of the coast-to-coast soup line problem mentioned above and the manner in which it drives outlay aggregates upward at mind-numbing speed. A worsening of the informal "misery index" (i.e. higher inflation and interest rates, or lower output growth and employment rates) drives hard on entitlements, indexing, debt servicing, budget authority spend-down rates, and loan facilities spread throughout the federal government, resulting in a surge of incremental outlays.

Between June and November, for example, federal outlay estimates have risen from $613 billion to $649 billion. Of the $36 billion growth in outlay estimates, fully *$26 billion or 72 percent* is due to automatic budget responses to the mechanisms listed above.

The $3.2 billion increment for interest outlays represents a revision of the 1981 average T-bill rate from *9.6 in June to 11.0* in the latest estimate. Similarly, the $9.2 billion increment for trade adjustment assistance, food stamps, cash assistance, and unemployment benefits represents a revised assumption about the expected *duration* of high unemployment during calendar 1981. The continuing disintermediation crisis in the thrift sector will cause nearly a billion dollar draw-down from the savings and loan insurance fund. Category (4) presents still another example of the soup line dynamic: when private sector orders soften, federal defense and "brick and mortar" contractors tend to

**Sources of $36 Billion Growth in FY 81 Outlay Estimates
Between June and November**

Program: Excess Cost Over June
                           (First) Budget Resolution

1) Due to Higher Inflation:
    Indexed Benefits:

Program		
Social Security	$0.75 billion	
Pension Benefits	0.40	
Specific Price Reestimates		
Defense Fuel Costs	1.20	
Medicare	1.90	
Food Assistance	1.65	
Subtotal		$5.90 billion

2) Due to Higher Interest Rates:

Student Loans	0.40	
Interest on the Debt	1.30	
Rural Housing Programs	0.15	
FSLIC Outlays	0.95	
Subtotal		2.80

3) Due to Higher Unemployment:

Medicaid	0.60	
Assistance Payments	0.75	
Unemployment Insurance	4.70	
TRA	2.10	
Food Stamps	0.30	
Federal Supplemental Unemployment Insurance Benefits	0.70	
Subtotal		9.15

4) Due to General Economic Conditions:

Defense Department Procurement	3.35	
Non-Defense Procurement	3.25	
Corps of Engineers	0.10	
EPA Sewer Construction	0.10	
VA Construction	0.10	
SBA Disaster Loans	1.35	
Subtotal		8.25
GRAND TOTAL		$26.10 billion

speed up delivery on contract work, increasing the spend-out rate against obligated authority in the pipeline—in this case by about $5 billion.

These illustrations drive home a fundamental point: achieving fiscal control over outlays and Treasury borrowing *cannot be conducted as an accounting exercise* or *exclusively through legislated spending cuts in the orthodox sense*. Only a comprehensive economic package that spurs output and employment growth and lowers *inflation expectations* and interest rates has any hope of stopping the present hemorrhage.

The deficit and total federal credit activity figures are even more alarming. When the off-budget deficit is included, which it must be since most of this category represents Treasury advances to the Federal Financing Bank (which in turn are financed in the government market for bonds and T-bills), the pre-tax cut deficit for FY 81 ranges between $50–60 billion.* This follows a closing level of nearly $80 billion for FY 80 (including off-budget).

The vigorous tax-cut package required to spur the supply side of the economy could raise the total static FY 81 deficit to the *$60–80 billion* range, depending upon the timing of tax-cut implementation and real GNP, employment, and inflation levels during the remaining nine months of the fiscal year. These parameters make clear that unless the tax-cut program is accompanied by a credible and severe program to curtail FY 81–82 outlays, future spending authority, and overall federal credit absorption, financial market worries about a "Reagan inflation" will be solidly confirmed by the budget posture.

An alternative indication of the fiscal management crisis is given by the figures for new loan and loan guarantee

---

*This assumes current estimate revenues of $615 billion, outlays of $649 billion, an on-budget deficit of $35 billion, and an off-budget deficit of $20 billion.

activities during FY 81 by federal agencies. These are now estimated at *$150 billion*, with only $44 billion of this amount included in the *official on-budget accounts*. Thus, federal credit agencies will absorb an additional *$100 billion* in available funds beyond the Treasury's requirements for financing the official deficit.

It is these spending growth trends, deficit levels, and federal credit absorption parameters which are generating market expectations of a chronic and severe Reagan inflation: market participants simply will not accept the Federal Reserve's money growth and anti-inflation goals in light of this massive governmental domination of credit markets.

4) Commodity Shocks and the Final Destruction of Volcker Monetary Policy

The U. S. economy is likely to face two serious commodity price run-ups during the next five-to-fifteen months. First, if the Iran–Iraq war is not soon terminated, today's excess worldwide crude and product inventories will be largely depleted by February or March. Under those conditions, heavy spot market buying, inventory accumulation, and eventually panic bidding on world markets will once again emerge. Indeed, unless the war combatants exhaust themselves at an early date and move quickly back into at least limited production, this outcome is almost certain by spring. Under these circumstances, OPEC contract rates will rise toward spot market levels in the $40–50 per barrel range during the first and second quarters of 1981, with a consequent price shock to the U.S. economy. Even a $10 per barrel increase in average U.S. refiner acquisition cost would add $50–60 billion annually to aggregate national petroleum expenditures (assuming full decontrol).

Similarly, the present rapid draw-down of worldwide feed grain and protein oil reserves could turn into a rout by the fall of 1981, if the Soviets have another "Communist" (i.e. poor) harvest, and production is average-to-below-average elsewhere in the world. Under an adverse, but not improbable, 1981 harvest scenario, $4–5 corn, $6–7 wheat, and $10–11 soybeans are a distinct possibility.

The problem here is that demand for these basic commodities is highly inelastic in the very short run; and this generates strong credit demands from both the business and household sectors to finance existing consumption levels without cutting back on other expenditures. If the Federal Reserve chooses to accommodate these commodity price/credit demand shocks, as it has in the past, then in the context of the massive federal credit demand and financial market disorders described above, only one result is certain: the *already tattered credibility of the post-October 1979 Volcker monetary policy will be destroyed*. The Federal Reserve will subsequently succumb to enormous internal strife and external pressure, and the conditions for full-scale financial panic and unprecedented global monetary turbulence will be present. The January economic package, therefore, must be formulated with these probable 1981 commodity shocks and resulting financial market pressures clearly in mind.

5) Ticking Regulatory Time Bomb

Unless swift, comprehensive and far-reaching regulatory policy corrections are undertaken immediately, an unprecedented, quantum scale-up of the much discussed "regulatory burden" will occur during the next eighteen-to-forty months. Without going into exhaustive detail, the basic dynamic is this: during the early- and mid-1970s, Congress approved more than a dozen sweeping environmental, energy, and safety enabling authorities, which for all practical purposes are devoid of policy standards and criteria for cost-benefit, cost-effectiveness, and comparative risk analysis. Subsequently, McGovernite no-growth activists assumed control of most of the relevant sub-Cabinet policy posts during the Carter Administration. They have spent the past four years "tooling up" for implementation through a mind-boggling outpouring of rule-makings, interpretative guidelines, and major litigation—all heavily biased toward maximization of regulatory scope and burden. Thus, this decade-long process of regulatory evolution is just now reaching the stage at which it will sweep through the industrial economy with near gale force, preempting multi-billions in investment capital, driving up operating costs, and siphoning off management and technical personnel in an incredible morass of new controls and compliance procedures.

In the auto manufacturing sector, for example, new if substantially tougher regulations in the following areas will impact the industry during 1981–84: passive restraint standard (airbags); 1981 passenger tailpipe standard (including an unnecessary 3.4 gram/mile CO limit); unproven five mph bumper standards; final heavy duty engine emission standards; vast new audit, enforcement, and compliance procedures, and a new performance warranty system; light duty diesel particulate and NO standards; heavy duty truck noise standards; model year 1983–85 light duty truck emission standards; MY 83–85 light duty truck fuel econo standards; bus noise standards; ad infinitum. These measures alone will generate $10–20 billion in capital and operating costs while yielding modest to non-existent social benefits.

Similarly, a cradle-to-grave hazardous waste control system under RCRA will take effect in 1981 at an annual cost of up to $2 billion. While prudent national waste disposal standards are clearly needed, the RCRA system is a *monument to mindless excess:* it treats degreasing fluids and PCBs in the same manner; and the proposed standards and controls for generators, transporters, and disposers, along with relevant explanations and definitions, encompass more than 500 pages of the Federal Register.

Multi-billion dollar overkill has also bloomed in the regulatory embellishment of the Toxic Substances Control Act, which threatens to emulate FDA "regulatory lag" on new chemical introductions. The proposed OSHA [Occupational Safety and Health Administration] generic carcinogen standard and the technology based BACT, RACT, LAER and NSPS standards under the Clean Air Act also represent staggering excess built upon dubious scientific and economic premises. Three thousand pages of appliance efficiency standards scheduled for implementation in thirteen categories of home appliances in 1981 also threaten to create multi-billion dollar havoc in the appliance industry.

There are also literally dozens of recently completed or still pending rule-makings targeted to specific sectors of the industrial economy as follows: proposed NSPS [New Source Performance Standards] standards for small industrial boilers (10–250 million BTU per hour) are estimated at $1–2 billion over 1980–85; proposed utility sector standards for bottom ash, fly ash, and cooling water control could cost $3.3 billion; pending OSHA hearing conservation standards, $500 million; abrasive blasting standards, $130 million; and asbestos control standards, up to $600 million. New industrial waste water pretreatment standards . . . EPA's proposed fluorocarbon-refrigerant control program . . . the CAA stage II vapor recovery and fugitive hydrocarbon control program . . . the vehicle inspection and maintenance program . . . all have price tags in excess of $1 billion. Moreover, most of the country will fail to meet the 1982 compliance deadline for one or more regulated air pollutants, thereby facing a potential absolute shut-down on the permitting of new or modified industrial sources. All told, there are easily in excess of *$100 billion in new environmental safety and energy compliance costs* scheduled for the early 1980s.

II.
THE THREAT OF POLITICAL DISSOLUTION

This review of the multiple challenges and threats lying in ambush contains an inescapable warning: things could go very badly during the first year, resulting in incalculable erosion of GOP momentum, unity, and public confidence. If bold policies are not swiftly, deftly, and courageously implemented in the first six months, Washington will quickly become engulfed in political disorder commensurate with the surrounding economic disarray. A golden opportunity for permanent conservative policy revision and political realignment could be thoroughly dissipated before the Reagan Administration is even up to speed.

The specific danger is this: if President Reagan does not lead a creatively orchestrated high-profile policy offensive based on revision of the fundamentals—supply-side tax-cuts and regulatory relief, stern outlay control and federal fiscal retrenchment, and monetary reform and dollar stabilization—the thin Senate Republican majority and the de facto conservative majority in the House will fragment and succumb to parochial "fire-fighting as usual" in response to specific conditions of constituency distress.

For example, unless the whole remaining system of crude oil price controls, refiner entitlements, gasoline allocations, and product price controls is administratively terminated "cold turkey" by February 1, there is a high probability of gasoline lines and general petroleum market disorder by early spring. These conditions would predictably elicit a desultory new round of Capitol Hill initiated energy policy tinkering reminiscent of the mindless exercises of Summer 1979. Intense political struggles would develop over implementation of the stand-by conservation programs, extension of EPAA controls and allocations, and funding levels for various pie-in-the-sky solar, conservation, synfuels, and renewables programs. The administration would lose the energy policy initiative and become engulfed in defensive battles, and frenetic energy legislating would preempt Hill attention from more important budget control, entitlement reform, and regulatory revision efforts. In short, if gas lines are permitted to erupt due to equivocation on revocation of controls, debilitating legislative and political distractions will be created.

Similarly, failure to spur early economic expansion and alter financial market inflation expectations will result in a plethora of Capitol Hill initiatives to "fix up" the housing, auto and steel sectors, hype up exports, subsidize capital formation, provide municipal fiscal relief, etc. Again, the Administration would be thrown on the defensive. Finally, persistence of "misery index"-driven budget deficits, high interest and inflation rates, and continued monetary policy vacillation at the Fed would quickly destroy the present GOP consensus on economic policy, pitting tax-cutters against budget-cutters and capital formation boosters against Kemp-Roth supporters.

To prevent early dissolution of the incipient Republican majority, only one remedy is available: an initial Administration economic program that is so bold, sweeping and sustained that it—

—totally dominates the Washington agenda during 1981;
—holds promise of propelling the economy into vigorous expansion and the financial markets into a bullish psychology;
—preempts the kind of debilitating distractions outlined above.

The major components and tenor of such an orchestrated policy offensive are described below.

III.
EMERGENCY ECONOMIC STABILIZATION AND RECOVERY PROGRAM

In order to dominate, shape, and control the Washington agenda, President Reagan should declare a national economic emergency soon after inauguration. He should tell the Congress and the nation that the economic, financial, budget, energy, and regulatory conditions he inherited are far worse than anyone had imagined. He should request that Congress organize quickly and clear the decks for *exclusive action* during the next hundred days on an *Emergency Economic Stabilization and Recovery Program* he would soon announce. The administration should spend the next two to three weeks in fevered consultation with Hill congressional leaders and interested private parties on the details of the package.

Five major principles should govern the formulation of the package:

1) A static "waste-cutting" approach to the FY 81 outlay component of the fiscal hemorrhage will hardly make a dent in the true fiscal problem. Persisting high "misery index" conditions in the economy will drive the soup line mechanisms of the budget faster than short-run, line-item cuts can be made on Capitol Hill. Fiscal stabilization (i.e. elimination of deficits and excessive rates of spending growth) can only be achieved by sharp improvement in the economic indicators over the next twenty-four months. This means that the policy initiatives designed to spur output growth and to lower inflation expectations and interest rates must carry a large share of

the fiscal stabilization burden. Improvement in the "outside" economic forces driving the budget is just as important as success in the "inside" efforts to effect legislative and administrative accounting reductions.

2) For this reason, dilution of the tax-cut program in order to limit short-run static revenue losses during the remainder of FY 81 and FY 82 would be counterproductive. Weak real GNP and employment growth over calendar years 1981 and 1982 will generate soup line expenditures equal to or greater than any static revenue gains from trimming the tax program.

3) The needed rebound of real GNP growth and especially vigorous expansion in the capital spending sector of the economy can not be accomplished by tax-cuts alone. A dramatic, substantial *recision* of the regulatory burden is needed both for the short-term cash flow relief it will provide to business firms and the long-term signal it will provide to corporate investment planners. A major "regulatory ventilation" will do as much to boost business confidence as tax and fiscal measures.

4) High, permanent inflation expectations have killed the long-term bond and equity markets that are required to fuel a capital spending boom and regeneration of robust economic growth. Moreover, this has caused a compression of the financial liability structure of business into the short-term market for bank loans and commercial paper, and has caused a flight of savings into tangible assets like precious metals, land, etc. The result of this credit market dislocation and inversion is that super-heated markets for short-term credits keep interest rates high and volatile and make monetary policy almost impossible to conduct.

The Reagan financial stabilization plan must seek to restore credit and capital market order and equilibrium by supporting monetary policy reform and removing the primary cause of long-term inflation pessimism: the explosive growth of out-year federal liabilities, spending authority, and credit absorption.

This points to the real leverage and locus for budget control: *severe recession of entitlement* and *new obligational authority* in the federal spending pipeline, which creates outlay streams and borrowing requirements in FY 82, FY 83, and beyond. The critical nature of *future spending authority* is dramatically illustrated by the experience during FY 1980: new budget authority increased from $556 billion (FY 79) to nearly $660 billion in FY 80, an increase of more than $100 billion, or 18 percent. Much of this authority will create outlay streams and Treasury cash borrowing requirements in FY 81 and beyond.

The fiscal stabilization package adopted during the hundred-day session, therefore, *must be at minimum equally weighted between out-year spending and entitlement authority reductions* and cash outlay savings for the remainder of FY 81. Indeed, the latter possibilities are apparently being exaggerated and over-emphasized. Of the current $649 billion FY 81 outlay estimate, $187 billion stems from prior year obligations or authority and cannot be stopped legally; $97 billion represents defense-spending from current obligations and should not be stopped; another $260 billion represents permanent authority primarily for Social Security and interest. The latter can only be reduced by "outside" economic improvements, and the former would be a political disaster to tinker with in the first round. This leaves $159 billion in controllable outlays, half of which will be spent or obligated before Congress acts in February–April. In short, $13 billion (2 percent) in waste-cutting type FY 81 cash outlay savings must be gotten from an $80 billion slice of the budget. Achieving this 16 percent hold-down will be tough and necessary, but if it is the primary or exclusive focus of the initial fiscal package, the ball game will be lost.

Again, the primary aim of the fiscal control component must be to shift long-term inflation expectations downward and restore bond and equity markets. Severe reductions in out-year authority and federal credit absorption can accomplish this. In turn, robust long-term capital markets would lessen the traffic jam in short-term credit markets by permitting corporate portfolio restructuring and by drawing savings out of unproductive tangible assets. The conditions for reestablishing monetary policy credibility would be achieved and short-term interest rates, demand for money and inflation expectations would adjust accordingly.

5) Certain preemptive steps must be taken early on to keep control of the agenda and to maintain Capitol Hill focus on the Stabilization and Recovery Program. Foremost, all remaining petroleum product controls and allocations should be cancelled on day one. This will prevent a "gasoline line crisis," but will permit retail prices to run up rapidly if the world market tightens sharply as expected. This prospective price run-up can be readily converted into an asset: it can provide the political motor force for a legislative and administrative program to set up U.S. energy program production (see below).

In addition, some informal agreement should be sought with Chairmen Hatch, Garn, and others to defer the labor policy agenda (minimum wage, Davis Bacon, etc.) until the fall of 1981. Both committees will have a substantial role in the stabilization program, and there is no point in antagonizing organized labor during this critical period. Similarly, the Moral Majority agenda should also be deferred. Pursuit of these issues during the hundred-day period would only unleash cross-cutting controversy and political pressures which would undermine the fundamental administration and congressional GOP economic task.

The following includes a brief itemization of the major components of the Stabilization and Recovery Program:

a) Supply-Side Tax Components

The calendar year 1981 and 1982 installments of Kemp-Roth, reduction of the top income tax rate on unearned income to 50 percent, further reduction in capital gains, and a substantial reform along 10–5–3 lines of corporate depreciation.

b) Fiscal Stabilization Component

This would consist of two parts. First, the cash outlay savings measures for the remainder of FY 81 would be aimed at holding outlays to the $635 billion range. A hiring freeze and a severe cutback in agency travel, equipment procurement, and outside contracting would be the major areas for savings.

The second part would be oriented toward entitlement revisions and budget authority reductions in FY 82 and beyond. Some of this could be accomplished through budget authority recisions included in the remainder of the FY 81 appropriations bill. This would have to be enacted before the expected December–March continuing resolution expires. Expiration of the continuing resolution would provide strong leverage. Another part could be accomplished through the revised FY 82 budget and scaled-back requests for new budget authority. The remainder would require the legislative committees to address a carefully tailored package of initial entitlement revisions.

Expressed in functional program and spending areas the out-year authority reduction package should address the following items, with a view to reducing federal domestic program levels by $30–50 billion per annum in the FY 82–83 period:

1) *Public sector capital investment deferrals.* We are now spending about $25 billion per year for highways, mass transit, sewer treatment facilities, public works, national parks, and airport facilities. These are all necessary and productive federal investments, but their benefit stream will accrue over the next twenty-to-forty years. In light of the current financial crisis, a modest deferral and stretchout of activity rates (a 10–20 percent reduction) in these areas should be considered.

2) *Non-Social Security entitlements.* Current expenditures for food stamps, cash assistance, Medicaid, disability, heating assistance, housing assistance, WIC, school lunches, and unemployment compensation amount to $100 billion. A carefully tailored package to reduce eligibility, overlap, and abuse should be developed for these areas—with potential savings of $10–20 billion.

3) *Low priority program cut-backs.* Total FY 81 expenditures for NASA, CETA, UDAG, the Community Development Program, EDA, urban parks, impact aid, Action, Department of Energy commercialization and information programs, arts and humanities, and the Consumer Cooperative Bank amount to $25 billion. Most of these programs are ineffective or of low priority and could be cut by at least one third or $8 billion.

4) *Federal credit, lending, and guarantee reform.* As was indicated previously, concessional direct lending and loan guarantee activities by on-budget, off-budget, and government-sponsored enterprises is now running rampant, absorbing ever bigger shares of available credit market funds. These programs are buried in HUD, SBA, FmHA, EDA, USDA, Commerce and HHS, as well as in the traditional housing credit and farm credit agencies. Controlling SBA direct grant activities, for instance, will accomplish little if program activity is simply shifted to concessional loan authorities, with the resultant outlays laundered through the FFB.

c) Regulatory Ventilation

This component also has two segments. The first and most urgent is a well-planned and orchestrated series of unilateral administrative actions to defer, revise, or rescind existing and pending regulations where clear legal authority exists. The potential here is really staggering, as this hastily compiled list of specific actions indicates. The important thing is that the workup on these initiatives must occur during the transition and very early after the inauguration. Again, the aim would be to firmly jolt business confidence and market psychology in a favorable direction.

These are suggestive illustrations with rough savings parameters from among literally dozens of potential unilateral administrative actions of this sort. A centralized Transition Task Force charged with identification of targets for early action and determination of required legal and rule-making procedures to commence after inauguration could help speed this initiative.

On a second front, both temporary and permanent statutory revisions will be needed. There are literally dozens of rulemaking and compliance deadlines on the statute books

Action	Impact
1) Grant model year 1982 CO waiver	$300 million auto industry savings
2) Rescind passive restraint standard	$300-600 million auto investment savings over three years
3) Relax 1984 heavy duty truck emission standard	Minimum savings of $100 million
4) Simplify auto emissions certification and testing	$80 million per year
5) Modify ambient air standard for ozone to permit multiple exceedences or higher standard value in conformance with scientific evidence	$15-40 billion in reduced compliance costs over next eight years
6) Eliminate unnecessary NSPS for small industrial boilers	$1-2 billion over next five years
7) Cancel EPA fuel additive testing program	Savings of $90-120 million
8) Relax proposed light duty truck emission standards for post-1983	Savings would be a substantial fraction of currently estimated $1.3 billion compliance cost
9) Modify or defer EPA pre-treatment standards for industrial waste-water	Savings of a substantial fraction of the $6 billion compliance cost for just three sectors—utilities, steel and paper
10) Cancel DOE appliance efficiency standards	Avoids multi-billion dollar havoc in an industry that is already improving product efficiency in response to market pressure
11) Eliminate building energy performance standards	Market forces are working here, too, but rigid BTU budgets for each new structure could cost billions per year for non cost-effective energy savings

Action	Impact
12) Modify RCRA to incorporate "degree of hazard" and control system simplification	Savings would be some fraction of $2 billion per year
13) Defer new OSHA workplace noise standards	Save $250 million per year
14) Modify or defer pending OSHA standards on scaffolding, asbestos exposure, cadmium and chromium exposure, and grain elevator dust control	More than $1 billion in annual combined savings

for the next twenty months that cannot be prudently met. An omnibus "suspense bill" might be necessary during the hundred-day session to defer these deadlines and to implement the one-year moratorium on new rule-makings proposed by Murray Wiedenbaum.

Finally, a fundamental legislative policy reform package to be considered after the hundred-day period will have to be developed. This would primarily involve the insertion of mandatory cost-benefit, cost-effectiveness, and comparative risk analyses into the basic enabling acts—Clean Air and Water, Safe Drinking Water, TOSCA, RCRA, OSHA, etc. Without these statutory changes, administrative rule-making revisions in many cases will be subject to successful court challenge.

d) Contingency Energy Package

The probable 1981 "oil shock" could entail serious political and economic disruption. Therefore, the preemptive step of dismantling controls before the crisis really hits is imperative. Incidentally, the combination of immediate decontrol and a $10 rise in the world price would increase windfall profits tax revenue by $20–25 billion during calendar 1981, thereby adding substantially to short-run budget posture improvement, if not to long-run energy production prospects.

But beyond this, a planning team should be readying a package of emergency steps to increase short-run domestic energy production and utilization. This should be implemented if the world market pinch becomes severe. The primary areas for short-run gains would be: accelerated licensing of a half-dozen completed nuclear plants; removal of all end-use restrictions on natural gas; changes in NGPA to permit accelerated infill drilling and near-term production gains; elimination of stripper, marginal and EOR oil properties from the windfall tax; emergency variances from SO_2 standards for industrial and utility coal boilers; and power wheeling from coal-nuclear to oil-based utility systems.

If the crisis is severe enough, rapid statutory revision of the natural gas decontrol program and modification of the windfall tax might be considered as part of the hundred-day agenda.

e) A Monetary Accord

The markets have now almost completely lost confidence in Volcker and the new monetary policy. Only an extraordinary gesture can restore the credibility that will be required during the next two years. President Reagan should meet with Volcker or the entire Federal Reserve Board at an early date and issue them a new informal "charter" —namely, to eschew all consideration of extraneous economic variables like short-term interest rates, housing market conditions, business cycle fluctuations, etc., and to concentrate instead on one exclusive task: bringing the growth of Federal Reserve credit and bank reserves to a prudent rate and stabilization of the international and domestic purchasing power of the dollar.

The President and Congress would jointly take responsibility for ameliorating credit and capital market conditions through implementation of the Stabilization and Recovery Program and would stoutly defend the Fed from all political attacks. Insulation of the Fed from extraneous economic and financial preoccupations, political pressures, recalibration of its monetary objective, and restoration of its tattered credibility is the critical lynch-pin in the whole program.

EXCERPTS FROM AN OFF-THE-RECORD DINNER ADDRESS BY DAVID STOCKMAN TO THE DIRECTORS OF THE NEW YORK STOCK EXCHANGE, JUNE 5, 1985

When the books close on this fiscal year next October 1 we will have run up another $200 billion in national debt. . . . Let me suggest two standards which apply equally to both sides in this monumental debate.

First, there is a plausible case for both going-in positions —no tax increases and no domestic spending cuts—but neither can be responsibly held unless one is willing to spell out and be politically accountable for the consequences on the other side of the budget ledger: No spending cuts mean drastic tax increases, and vice versa.

Secondly, as the fiscal crisis has worsened and the political conflict intensified, we have increasingly resorted to squaring the circle with accounting gimmicks, half-truths and downright dishonesty in our budget numbers, debate and advocacy.

On the second standard, honesty in accounting, we have not come entirely clean. The Senate Budget rests on some pretty optimistic assumptions about the path of our economy over the next three years—namely 4 percent average growth over the next fourteen quarters, inflation where it is and a steady descent of interest rates to 5.5 percent on Treasury bills by 1988.

My point is this: Reasonable people can say the $10 billion is all we wish to take out of domestic spending and $20–$25 billion is what we plan to take out of defense. But reasonable people must also acknowledge that $20–$25 billion in higher taxes are then necessary to be consistent with fiscal sanity.

As a policy matter, it is obvious enough that to close this threatening $200 billion budget gap, we must either massively cut spending or raise taxes by large, unprecedented magnitudes—or, by the lights of some, enact a sweeping mixture of both.